The Traveler's Guide to Native America

The Southwest Region

WITHDRAWN

By Hayward Allen

NORTHWORD
PRESS, INC.
P.O. Box 1360, Minocqua, WI 54548

Library of Congress Cataloging-in-Publication Data

Allen, Hayward
   A traveler's guide to Native America. The Southwest region / by
Hayward Allen.
      p. cm. -- (Origins ; 2nd)
   ISBN 1-55971-158-2 : $16.95
   1. Indians of North America--Southwest, New--History--Guidebooks.
2. Indians of North America--Southwest, New--Antiquities-
-Guidebooks. 3. Southwest, New--Antiquities--Guidebooks.
4. Southwest, New--Guidebooks. I. Title. II. Series: Origins
(Minocqua, Wis.) ; 2nd.
   E78.S7A475 1993
   917.9--dc20   93-15265
                                                       CIP

CREDITS

Front cover photograph: Aimee Madsen
Back cover photograph: Reinhard Brucker

Inside photographs

Reinhard Brucker, pp. 10-11, 14, 16, 20, 21, 22, 23, 26, 28, 29, 33, 34, 35, 36, 40, 45, 46, 50, 54, 65, 70, 87, 90, 93, 97, 98, 100, 108, 109, 112, 113, 114, 115, 116, 118, 119, 134, 136, 137, 138, 140, 141, 142, 143, 144, 147, 151, 155, 156, 159, 166, 170, 171, 172, 174, 177, 178, 182; Carol Christensen, p. 173; Kenji Kawano, pp. 4-5, 6, 30, 38, 41, 43, 44, 48, 53, 59, 81, 84, 103, 104, 105, 110, 121, 122, 124, 127, 175; Martin Kleinsorge, pp. 37, 91; Thomas Maxwell, p. 153.

© 1993 Hayward Allen. All rights reserved.
Published by NorthWord Press, Inc.
Box 1360, Minocqua, WI 54548

Edited by Greg Linder
Designed by Russell S. Kuepper

For a free catalog describing NorthWord's
line of nature books and gifts, call 1-800-336-5666.

ISBN 1-55971-158-2

DEDICATION

This wonderful journey would not have turned wheels without the encouragement and support of Pat and Tom. Ronda Lyon Allen walked every step along the paths and trails, not only pointing out aspects I did not see but also being a caretaker of the many sacred places. She became the representative con-science of the sensitive traveler. She immersed herself in the enthusiasm of being a discoverer of those cultures represented in this volume of *ORIGINS*. This shared wonder, after so many trips, caused us to create a home in Arizona. What began as exploration in an exotic land became a journey that led us home.

TABLE
OF CONTENTS

NATIVE AMERICA: The Basics

For the uninitiated traveler, here is fundamental information about today's Native Americans, adapted from the Bureau of Indian Affairs publication, *American Indians Today—Answers to Your Questions*.

Who are Indians (Native Americans)?

To be designated as a Native American eligible for basic Bureau of Indian Affairs services, an individual must live on or near a reservation, or on or near trust or restricted land under the jurisdiction of the Bureau; be a member of a tribe, band, or group of Indians recognized by the federal government; and for some purposes, be of one-fourth or more Indian descent.

How does a Native American become a member of a tribe?

By meeting membership requirements laid down by the tribe or through adoption by the tribal governing body according to rules established by the tribe. The amount of Indian blood needed varies with the tribe. It ranges from a trace to as much as one-half.

What is an Indian reservation?

An area of land for Indian use. The name comes from the early days of Indian-white relationships when Indians relinquished land through treaty, "reserving" a portion for their own use. Reservations have been created by treaties, Congressional acts, executive orders, and agreements.

Do all Native Americans live on reservations?

No. Approximately one-half of Native Americans live off reservations.

Are Native Americans wards of the government?

The federal government is a trustee of Indian property, but Native Americans are not wards of the government, nor is the government the guardian of the individual Native American.

Do Native Americans get payments from the government?

There is no payment to a person because he is a Native American. Payments may be made to Indian tribes or individuals for losses which resulted from treaty violations or encroachments upon lands or interests reserved to the tribe by the government. Tribes or individuals may receive government checks for income from their land and resources, but only because the assets are held in trust by the Secretary of the Interior and payment for the use of the Indian resource has been collected by the federal government.

Are Native Americans citizens?

Yes. The Congress, on June 2, 1924, extended American citizenship to all Native Americans born within the territorial limits of the United States.

May Native Americans vote?

Yes, on the same basis as other citizens of their respective states. Qualifications for voting in Indian tribal elections, however, have no relationship to the right of the Native American to vote in national, state, or local elections open to citizens in general. So far as tribal elections are concerned, voting rights may be restricted by tribal resolutions or ordinances.

May Native Americans own property?

Yes, they may. Indian lands are owned by Indian tribes and individual Indians. Nearly all the lands of Indian tribes, however, are held by the United States in trust for a particular tribe, and there is no general law that will permit the tribe to sell its land. Individual Indian lands are also held in trust. However, upon his request, a Native American may sell his land if the Secretary of the Interior or his representative determines this is in his long-range best interest.

Do Native Americans pay taxes?

Yes. They pay local, state, and federal taxes the same as other citizens unless a treaty, agreement, or statute exempts them. Most tax exemptions which have been granted apply to lands held in trust for Indians and to income from such land.

Do laws that apply to the non-Indian apply to the Native American as well?

The Native American, like the non-Indian, is in general subject to federal, state, and local law—unless he is on an Indian reservation. There, only federal and tribal laws apply, unless the Congress has provided otherwise. On reservations where only federal and tribal laws apply, federal jurisdiction is limited, applying to a limited number of more serious offenses. The great body of lesser crimes, however, is solely within the jurisdiction of tribal courts. Where tribes have failed to establish codes of laws and tribal courts, a code of offenses and an Indian court have been provided by the Secretary of the Interior.

Do Native Americans have their own governments?

Most do. The governing body of the tribe is generally referred to as the tribal council, and is made up of council members elected by vote of the adult members of the tribe and presided over by tribal chairpersons. The tribal council elected in this way has authority to speak and act for the tribe, and to represent it in negotiations with federal, state, and local governments.

Are Indian ceremonies open to the public?

The majority are. Some, however, are closed, primarily for religious reasons.

Are tourists welcomed on reservations?

Not all reservations have activities, attractions, or amenities for tourists. To determine what is available, contact the tribal council or tribal headquarters.

FOREWORD

Native America in the Southwest can provide the traveler with a splendid variety of imagination-provoking experiences. Too, we all carry with us snapshots, memories, and myths concerning the Southwest, and nearly all of these fit within two destinations: the Colorado Plateau, and the Four Corners region.

The Four Corners area is easily defined, for there is only one point in the contiguous United States where four states geometrically coincide: at the junction of Arizona, New Mexico, Colorado, and Utah. Here, if you dance or hop quickly enough, you can "reside" in four states within 30 seconds or less. Naturally (and nationally), it is a tourist attraction, with all the accompanying shops and southwestern paraphernalia.

The Colorado Plateau may be a less specific destination, but its significance emerges repeatedly throughout this book, as we seek to describe the lives and the cultures of the people who first called the area "home." The flowage of rivers, streams, and creeks, and the natural sculpting of escarpments within the Colorado Plateau reveal many reasons why native people at varying times ranged or settled on the high plains. The plains have assumed great social and spiritual meaning for the people who have lived upon them.

In a vehicle other than an airplane, it's possible for the traveler to create an itinerary that can, over a period of days, weeks, or months, provide great insight into the nature and history of the Southwest. Thousands of years of human history can be examined within a relatively brief time, and this is the primary excitement that awaits visitors to southwestern Native America. One of the goals of *The Traveler's Guide* is to provide some understanding of native history in each area, as well as guiding visitors to contemporary sites, events, and attractions.

Non-Indian as well as Indian travelers are often unaware of the cultural heritage of places with which they are not familiar. And despite the cornucopia of information available about different eras, areas, and peoples in the Southwest, it can be difficult to gain real insight without devoting a lifetime to study. We hope to at least offer preliminary insights, pointing readers in directions they may or may not choose to pursue.

There are dominant cultures in the Southwest—"superstars" like the Anasazi, the Hopi, or the Navajo. On the other hand, there are small groups that are barely afforded the luxury of a federal reservation. All of these cultures resulted from the area's historical construction. Layer upon layer, like the sandstone sculptures found near Sedona, Arizona, various "deposits" of human settlement arrived. For the most part, they stayed in the Southwest, and each contributed to the region's heritage.

You'll find a great deal of "ancient" history in this book. However, this should not give you the impression that Native America in the Southwest has come and is gone. It is precisely that history that can provide the traveler with the impetus to keep moving down those long roads leading to some of the most distant horizons to be found in our nation. That history is what many travelers are seeking, because it offers a vital connection between what has vanished and what remains. Simply put, we understand ourselves and our world better as we come to understand the past.

Yet we don't have to begin with or confine ourselves to the past. Learning about the contemporary Hopi, Pueblo, Zuni, Pima, Tohono O'Odham, Mohave, Pai, and other peoples will also reveal intricate footpaths that lead us to the ancient cultures. All times, it seems, lead to all other times.

This guide begins with Arizona, then moves on to New Mexico. These two states roughly include the areas that have long dominated Native American life in the Southwest. What has happened within the two states has spawned entire libraries devoted to archaeology, anthropology, and the cultural history of the region.

However, Colorado and Utah have played their own roles. Perhaps they were the backbone that reached above the ice floes, challenging the earliest people on their movement south. There is no doubt that the Utah-Colorado area held "outposts" of the Anasazi civilization, and emerging evidence suggests that Colorado may yet prove to be the Southwest's most significant Anasazi homeland. Both states have been home to tribal entities that would profoundly influence American Indian life.

Together, the states of Arizona, New Mexico, Colorado, and Utah—the "Four Corners" region—offer the thoughtful traveler in Native America an unparalleled opportunity to see, to learn, and to know.

—*Hayward Allen, 1993*

ARIZONA

Travelers to Arizona may go there for many reasons: business, pleasure, recreation, climate, or retirement. They may be just passing through on the way to El Paso or Los Angeles. Whatever the reason, it's almost impossible to visit the state without encountering what remains of ancient cultures—the Mogollon, the Anasazi, or the Hohokam cultures.

A mere two-hour layover at Phoenix's Sky Harbor Airport can provide an opportunity to visit some of the most unique historic sites to be found anywhere in the nation.

NAMING NAMES

We do not know what Arizona's first residents called the area in which they lived for generation after generation. Because we're not certain what these people called themselves, others have named them.

Hohokam, for example, is the Pima way of speaking about "the Vanished Ones," the people who long ago disappeared from places we now call Pueblo Grande or Casa Grande (which of course are Spanish names). In fact, *Pima* itself is the Spanish corruption of the Ah-kee-mult-o-o-tam words "pi-nyi-match," which is what the people said in response to questions posed by early missionaries and conquistadors.

It means "I don't know."

This linguistic conundrum applies to almost all Native American tribal and place names. *Ah-kee-mult-o-o-tam* translates into "river people," a name that distinguished those people from their neighbors, the *Tohono O'odham*, or "desert people." Travelers to Arizona will quickly understand why groups described themselves in terms of either the local geography or their histories.

The second major group of people who were among the first residents are termed the *Anasazi*, a term used by the Navajo (who call themselves Dineh, and their land Dinetah) to describe "Old Enemies."

The Hopi, truly named *Hopituh*, which means "the peaceful people," refer to the Anasazi as the Hisatsinom, or "Our Ancestors." Incidentally, the Hopi called the Dineh people the *Tavasuh*, which translates roughly into "head smashers," a reference to the way their neighbors tended to vanquish enemies. "Navajo" itself is a Pueblo word that refers to an area of land southwest of what is now called the Colorado River.

A Navajo shepherd tends his flock in Monument Valley.

Often it was only through names that people were able to designate where they lived, how they lived, and who their enemies and friends were. For example, the third group of early residents were the *Mogollon*, or "Mountain People." These Native Americans lived in the high valley area of what is now central and southern Arizona and New Mexico.

Although both the Anasazi and the Hohokam became known for their architectural and agricultural advances, there are those who believe that the Mogollon were the first to move from hunting-gathering subsistence to domesticated agrarian practices. They may also have been the first to build standardized pit homes, and to establish social and religious dwellings. Perhaps as a result of early contact with the Anasazi, they also created multi-structural villages.

The Mogollon culture's apex is generally considered to stretch from 300 B.C. to about 1400 A.D. They are thought to be descendants of the earlier Cochise people (not to be confused with the famed Apache leader), and it's believed that their lifeblood still runs through Zuni veins.

Petroglyphs carved by the Anasazi in Monument Valley depict bighorn sheep.

HOHOKAM CULTURE

Just a short cab ride from the Phoenix airport, the traveler can visit the Pueblo Grande Museum and Cultural Park, a unique inner-city historic monument.

Pueblo Grande, or "large village," was deserted for unknown reasons around 1450 A.D. (as were many other Hohokam villages). It was one of the area's most unique, most ambitious, and most inventive developments. The Hohokam people were farmers, but their feats of agricultural engineering set them apart from their neighbors.

The Hohokam were builders of canals. At some point long ago, someone decided that they could make the desert work *for* them instead of against them. This person undoubtedly suggested a way to make their harvests of corn, squash, beans, sunflowers, and even cactus more productive and less dependent upon seasonal whims.

The Hohokam created what became an elaborate network of canals and water gates that channeled the waters of the Salt, the Verde, and the Gila rivers into the people's fields. The channels became a political tool; whoever controlled the flow through the gates also had power over agricultural success or failure. A visit to the museum grounds will reveal to the traveler the profound meaning of this early decision to control the physical environment.

Pueblo Grande was once locally known as Snake City because a rattlesnake colony claimed title to the place and plagued archaeologists in the 1930s. When Phoenix city engineers began planning and building canals to distribute the Southwest's most valuable resource—water—they found that their excavations followed the canals of the Hohokam. The Hohokam had been there first, and they most assuredly knew what was needed for their own communities.

One of the special features of the Pueblo Grande Museum and Cultural Park is the evidence of what is called a "ball court." When the Spanish arrived in Central America in the 1500s, their diarists recorded an athletic competition involving a solid, rubber-gum ball. It weighed about six pounds, and various teams tried to keep the ball aloft and bounce it off a specially-sloped wall in the ball court. There was even a hoop or ring set vertically into the wall. According to these Spanish sports reporters, players were allowed to use only their hips, knees, and elbows to keep the ball in play. The resemblance to later Native American sports such as lacrosse is clear.

Pueblo Grande has such a sloped wall coupled with a circular arena or court. The museum also has samples of the rubber balls that were used, plus photographs of the Mesoamerican "hoop" that was used when the Spanish arrived. The continuous exchange of goods and cultural practices between Native American groups also carried athletics north to the Hohokam people.

In truth, the Mogollon and Anasazi peoples are the ones generally associated with Arizona, in both history and fiction. Yet the Hohokam might be called the "technological" link to the descendants of the two better-known cultures. The Hohokam were called "the Vanished Ones," "the Old Ones," or "All Used Up," in different translations of tribal languages. They may have disappeared or migrated; perhaps they were killed or assimilated. In any case, their legacy remains, and sites are readily accessible to the traveler.

An hour south of Phoenix sits Casa Grande Ruins National Monument, located just beyond the borders of the Gila River Pima-Papago Reservation. While this site is a fascinating remnant of Hohokam culture, it has also been roofed-over to protect the major ruin. What makes it different from other Hohokam locations is the material used to create a massive, high-rise, four-story structure.

Here the Hohokam dug a few feet below the surface of the desert and found a remarkably cohesive, clay-like earth that congealed into the density of concrete. By contrast, limestone rocks were used as the primary building material at Tuzigoot; at Wupatki, the native sandstone slab layers provided perfect building blocks. And at the totally misnamed Montezuma Castle, north of Phoenix, both resources were used. Continuing north and east, sites like Canyon de Chelly and Mesa Verde reveal that builders added the use of natural caves as the back walls and the sandstone overhang as a secondary roof to protect them from the elements.

Casa Grande was named by Father Kino, a Spanish missionary on a burro, who dropped by in 1694 en route to a more populous destination. It's a place where the traveler can appreciate the Gila River Hohokam canal system, which once extended for over 250 miles throughout the area. The indentations of many of these canals can still be seen by undertaking a close examination or by flying over the site. The Casa Grande Museum contains further evidence of the Hohokam culture's accomplishments.

According to archaeological hypotheses, Casa Grande was pivotal in the region for about a century, from 1350 to 1450 A.D. It is a modest but provocative national monument. There is even evidence of the universal need to leave one's name, rank, and serial number behind, including the scratchings of 19th-century U.S. cavalrymen who once patrolled the area.

The Pima-Papago live nearby on their reservation, and one of the Hohokam culture's chief crops, cotton, is still prevalent in the valley. Half a century ago, the water table was about ten feet below the ground surface. As the century closes, water sits about 100 feet below the surface. What was once a matter of digging by hand now requires expensive drilling.

The Hohokam did not limit their territorial and agricultural expansion to the flatlands of Phoenix and the Gila River's relatively level watershed. Something—expanded population, sapped-out soils, or perhaps more aggressive sub-tribal units— sent the Hohokam into what we now call the Verde Valley, or "Green Valley," then even farther north to the area called Sunset Crater, near present-day Flagstaff.

It's not difficult to understand why a progressive society might expand its territory. The success of the Hohokam experience filled their coffers and storehouses. Their systems allowed them a high degree of economic control and sustained production. It's no wonder that they looked for more "infertile" ground that could be made productive, and attempted to spread an increasing population that stretched available resources.

The Hohokam vanished from their new homelands within a century or so; perhaps they were more enthusiastic than was warranted by the environment. Yet in following their move up-country from what is now the Phoenix area, travelers can discover much evidence of Hohokam ingenuity. It's thought that the Hohokam came to the Verde Valley around 600 A.D. The people who later lived in the area were called *Sinagua* by the Spanish, a term that translates as "without water."

Two national monuments reflect the life of the Sinaguan and the Hohokam. At Montezuma Castle we witness the application of Hohokam engineering. Here, water was diverted from Beaver Creek into canals that rationed water into fields. The "Castle," misnamed by early Spanish settlers who didn't know the difference between Aztec and Sinaguan cultures, is actually an 1100 A.D. Sinaguan construction, but Hohokam canals and archaeological remnants are found here. Meanwhile, the Sinaguan people had learned different technologies— some from the Hohokam, and some from the Anasazi. Nearby is Montezuma Well, a similarly misnamed, spring-fed source of water for the Sinaguans. When conditions were unusually dry, water was carried in

pots to nourish the Sinaguan fields.

Just north of the valley is a wonderful site called Tuzigoot National Monument. *Tuzigoot* is an Apache word for "crooked water," which describes a creekbed that the Sinaguan people used to irrigate their fields at about the same time they were working Beaver Creek about 50 miles to the south. At Tuzigoot one finds a utilization of local resources that rivals any civilization that used different-shaped rocks from the locale and cemented them together to create buildings. If the traveler seeks contemporary parallels visible from Tuzigoot, the "ghost town" of Jerome—now a popular arts and crafts center—can be seen on a distant hillside from the monument. Jerome itself merits a visit, as it was one of the first of the territory's copper-mining communities, and for a time was Arizona's largest city. Many of the town's buildings resemble very closely the Sinaguan dwellings in the valley below.

ABOVE: *Ruins at Tuzigoot National Monument were constructed of local stones cemented together.*

LEFT: *Montezuma's Castle reflects both Sinaguan architecture and Hohokam engineering.*

21

Another national monument, this one called Sunset Crater, takes us even further back in history. At one time there were about 400 active volcanoes in the area, and Sunset Crater is a remnant of the last of these geological dramas. It erupted in about 1064, and one can easily imagine what the local people felt about the event.

It seems that just about everyone in the area wanted to see what the eruption was all about after everything cooled off. The Anasazi made their way to the vicinity, as did the Sinaguans, who had been living near the volcano when it erupted. They were joined by Hohokam farmers plus some Mogollon, Hopi, and even Patayan people from the south. They discovered that the widely distributed ash also greatly improved agricultural production, and for a while the groups lived cooperatively and peacefully.

The Sinaguans, noted as pithouse builders, learned to utilize the flat sandstone of the area to build pueblo-style constructions. Today's traveler can find evidence of these settlements about 15 miles north of the crater, at a site known as Wupatki National Monument. Of the ruins here, about 800 structures have been found and several have been excavated. Most, though, have not been disturbed.

The Lomaki Ruins is one of the many intriguing sites at Wupatki National Monument.

These native peoples stayed in the area for about 150 years before leaving for unknown reasons. It's interesting although probably coincidental that the last of the people left Wupatki around 1225 A.D. At about the same time, the five-story Montezuma Castle structure was being built on a cliff along Beaver Creek. For two centuries the people used what they had learned from the Anasazi who were expert cliff-dwelling builders and used the agricultural technology of the Hohokam. They then left and went elsewhere. This is a pattern that is prevalent in the early southwestern cultures.

The evacuation could have resulted from successive drought years—the excavation at Wupatki's major ruin reveals in their garbage and trash pits that lean years forced lean diets of yucca, while lush times left evidence of squash, corn, beans, and so forth. The exit of the original residents could also have been due to competition for fertile land with people who did not mind instigating warfare as a means of gaining ground. There is enough evidence to indicate that the more aggressive people, known today as the Yavapai and Apache, forced the Sinaguans to move north to join the equally peaceful people we now know as the Hopi.

Montezuma Well, misnamed by the Spanish, provided a spring-fed water source for the Sinaguans.

MOGOLLON CULTURE

To examine the Mogollon, or "Mountain People," it is necessary to consider what are thought to be their antecedents, the Cochise, who are generally thought to be the first peoples of the Southwest to "settle down" and become farmers, build houses, and make pottery. The people who study "prehistoric" cultures call groups like the Cochise "Archaic Indians," meaning those who foraged as a sustaining lifestyle. We can find evidence of the Cochise people in what is known as the "core area," the Great Desert Basin of the Southwest. From about 7000 B.C. until 1000 B.C., the Cochise lived on the shores of this huge lake, an inland sea. The water evaporated and faded into clouds above what we now think of as desert land. Like all people seeking survival, the Cochise moved away. In small groups they left their shrinking, once marvelously rich lake. They moved to the mesas and mountains, living in caves and under canyon walls.

The Cochise people lived according to the seasons. They searched the growing desert for flora and fauna they could eat, store, weave with, and otherwise use for their sustenance. Even the desert could produce good and useful plants and sustain its share of animals that also knew how to survive. The Cochise milled natural grains and vegetables, and succeeding cultures would use almost identical "manos" and "matates," grinding stones, arrows, and spear points—as tools to sustain their own lives. It is quite important to point out the value of these tools, for the people came to realize that they could survive on an arid land.

The Cochise also realized they could create their own caves by digging pits or using natural ones and then laying a roof over the place to keep out the elements, the greatest of which were sun and wind. They were also able to develop the technology to make pottery, useful as utensils and as spiritually significant figurines. They made talisman-like objects, perhaps toys for youngsters, out of split twigs or willow wands. For example, a deer talisman was found in the Grand Canyon that dates around 2500 B. C.

Adapting their lives to the higher elevations, the Mogollon descendants of the Cochise people continued to forage, but mixed their seasonal ventures to include harvestable crops like corn, beans, squash, tobacco, and cotton. Like some mountain cultures today, the Mogollon used a digging stick as their primary tool. Any examination of archaeological displays at the many Arizona museums, such as the Museum of Northern Arizona in Flagstaff, reveals just how small some of the early hunting weapons were, for around 500 A.D. the bow and arrow became a Mogollon device for hunting small game, including birds and little animals. The miniature size of the arrowhead also demonstrates the skill level of tribal hunters. Revealing as well is their skillful use of the boomerang as a means of hunting rabbits, and wooden slings that propelled pointed shafts.

The Mogollon buildings were elaborations of the Cochise pit houses, and were built in established village complexes. Dug a meter or so into the ground, they had log frames and complex roofing. Another element enters here that will become a feature of many Southwestern cultures—the pit structure that has spiritual significance, known as the "kiva." Also significant to almost all groups is the fact that while "doors" might allow movement from room to room, general entry to the structure was from the roof, via a ladder. Later the Anasazi will adapt Mogollon construction to above-ground dwellings, as well as multiple dwellings that not only accommodate increased family size but also extended family relationships—i.e., villages.

No doubt these developments over the centuries were the result of increasing populations, increased contacts with other peoples in the region, and the influences that resulted. One of the most treasured aspects—because of its rarity—is the development of Mogollon pottery. Tightly coiling ropes of clay and smoothing them together on the surface, the Mogollon applied a slip of liquid clay before the pot was fired. As cultural exchange continued, the Mogollon also began to paint upon their pottery. Artifacts produced by one particular sub-group, the Mimbres, have become perhaps the most sought-after of early pottery finds, for their black-on-white designs are so stunning and delicate as to make one wish there were a hidden cave somewhere in Arizona or New Mexico where a thousand pots simply awaited discovery and reverence.

Because they lived on varied terrains and in opposing climates, the Mogollons were also weavers. They used cotton, they used feathers, and they used fur-based yarn to create blankets and clothing. They also created wonderful and rare baskets, as well as objects made of bone, shells, and wood.

When did the Mogollon culture end? As in all things Native American, nothing ever truly leaves the cultural loop. Much of what is considered Mogollon can be found in later tribal groups such as the Anasazi, then later the Hopi, and specifically the Zuni.

ANASAZI CULTURE

If there is any one group that defines Arizona's role in the Colorado Plateau or the Four Corners area, despite all that we have described, that group is the Anasazi culture. Western archaeologists and anthropologists estimate that the Anasazi evolved on the scene around 500 B.C.

Geologically, that scene included the mesas, deep valleys, winding canyons, and wide plains of what is today southern Colorado, southeastern Utah, northwestern New Mexico, and the upper northern portion of Arizona. The Anasazi may have used the same kind of pit houses used by the Mogollon, and they certainly were aware of the architecture of the Hohokam and Sinaguan peoples. However, if we are looking for an antecedent of what we call the Pueblo people today, it is the Anasazi. Architecture is a key identifying factor, as is pottery and location of domestic sites. However grand the Casa Grande is, it is no real rival to the condo-apartment constructions of the Anasazi in some of the most remote areas of the American continent.

This petroglyph, found in Petrified Forest National Park, is one of many remnants of the Anasazi.

So remote, in fact, that it was a cowboy looking for strays who found what is called the Mesa Verde ruins in Colorado about a century ago. So remote that Chaco Canyon in New Mexico and Canyon de Chelly contain ruins in areas still being used by Navajo farmers and herders.

Photographers such as Edward Curtis, novelists such as Tony Hillerman, and essayists like Frank Waters have added to the glory and the fascination of the sites. Their work has also drawn potentially destructive tourists to these sites.

It is not important, at least today, to know what "The People" called themselves. As mentioned earlier, they were granted social and historic recognition by the Navajo/Dineh, who called them "Old Enemies." Western science generally places the Anasazi civilization from 100 B C. through about 1250 A.D. by using sophisticated analysis of logs used in construction. The major focus of today's travelers, though, is upon the ruins at places like Canyon de Chelly in Arizona, Mesa Verde in Colorado, and Chaco Canyon in New Mexico, and in some remote areas of Utah.

What we discover at such sites are "high-population zones," ones that numbered in the thousands, where the Anasazi people lived for at least a millennium in varied locations high and low, on mesa tops and in river valleys. The fact that they "vanished" like the Hohokam, the Mogollon, and the Sinaguan peoples makes their past even more romantic.

Part of this historic romanticism is due to the endurance of Anasazi architecture, which allowed artifacts almost as varied as Egyptian ruins to survive and be available for our viewing or study. There is no doubt either that the Anasazi eventually became other existing groups, mainly the Pueblo peoples, but the fact that the Hopi claim direct ancestral connection to them adds special meaning.

The traveler in Native America, especially in the Southwest, will find an endless, subject-specific selection of books and pamphlets about the early peoples—the Anasazi, the Hohokam, the Mogollon, the Sinaguan, etc. Every national park visitor's center or monument has its own museum or display area, and every public or private museum does as well. Travel the Southwest and you'll find that even the modern versions of the trading post will have reference books and pamphlets for sale.

SALADO CULTURE

The Salado people have not been mentioned thus far, in part because they are a shorter durational culture without the aesthetic appeal to collectors of the Mogollon, the Hohokam, the Anasazi, or even the Sinaguan peoples. The Spanish defined them according to their location, *salado* meaning "salty," a description of an arid homeland filled with salt licks and salt runs. Even though their history is somewhat obscure, the Salado people merit recognition.

The traveler should spend time at the Tonto National Monument. The name is misleading (it unfortunately recalls the *Lone Ranger* television and radio serial), but this site encapsulates what Native American life was like at about 1100 A.D. in the Southwest. At about that time, the Salado people built the settlement we now call Tonto National Monument.

The ruins at Tonto National Monument offer a picture of what life was like for the Salado around 1100 A.D.

Do not disregard this place. Do not confuse it with other places that, after a while, look alike. There is as much difference between Tonto and Tuzigoot as between Brooklyn and Boston.

Tonto National Monument tells its own story, and its chief characters are the Salado people. These farming people made their home next to the area near Tonto Creek, which flows into the Salt River. Here they lived in peaceful coexistence with the Hohokam people, who were already farming the area through irrigation. About 200 years later, the Salado moved from the valley into the cliffs and caves nearby. Here they built structures not unlike those found at Mesa Verde or Montezuma Castle, but the structures were inhabited for only about 50 years. Then, like so many native groups, the Salado moved on. The ruins of their constructions form the Tonto National Monument. A museum at the site showcases the distinctive pottery and exceptional weaving of the Salado people.

Montezuma Castle is nestled into the cliffs near Beaver Creek.

MOVING ON

Like the cultures themselves, we must move on to other peoples and more recent generations. One of the purposes of this book is that of sustaining a sense of cultural continuity. In fact, the magic of the Four Corners and the Colorado Plateau is not that we have places to visit, but that we can in effect walk the paths of history.

Let us move forward to the next generation of peoples. First, the Hopi. Second, the Navajo. Third, the Apache. Then we'll consider the exceptional range of Native American nationalities that call Arizona home. The state abounds not only in earlier settlements but in contemporary peoples whose lives reflect and respect their ancestors and antecedents.

HOPI CULTURE

It is important that travelers in this antique land understand the wisdom, the philosophy, and the geological relevance of the history of the Hopi. These people call the Anasazi "Our Ancestors," and their Creation stories place them here for thousands of years. Western science disagrees, but that's not surprising. Anyone who has a fundamental interest in history will appreciate the fascinating differences and similarities between scientific and religious descriptions of time. In visiting this portion of southwestern Native America, the traveler will encounter both visions of history, and is well-advised to regard each with respect.

Numerous tourist-oriented or anthropological books deal with Hopi culture and history. Perhaps the best guide to the Hopi people of the First, Second, and Third Mesas is the *Book of the Hopi*, edited and compiled by Frank Waters. Excellent photographic evidence comes from Edward Curtis, whose early 20th-century photogravure illustrations of Hopi life may be the most valid images available to the non-Hopi. The Hopi are a culturally protective people.

During his three-year project, Frank Waters lived in a small Hopi dwelling below Pumpkin Seed Point. He was offered food and subsistence by Oswald and Naomi White Bear Fredericks, who lived a half-mile away. For Waters' benefit (and now our own) White Bear interpreted Hopi life and history, as told by 30 Hopi elders.

When one travels through the various "countries" of Arizona, each and every one corresponds exactly with what the Hopi describe in Waters' book. At the same time, two aspects of the culture become apparent. One is the secretive nature of the Hopi people and their strict sense of privacy. The traveler is not allowed even to photograph signs that identify Hopi towns and villages, and cannot attend the sacred dances and ceremonies. Although such prohibitions may seem rigid and unfriendly to some, they serve to protect and preserve all that is important about Hopi culture. When the traveler has the rare and unexpected chance to visit the Hopi in their homes or on the Three Mesas, it's imperative to abide by all their rules and expectations of respect. The reward lies in a visit to a native culture that remains virtually intact.

The Three Mesas area is so close to the Grand Canyon and the Rio Grande and Verde valleys, so near to magnificent ruins and almost indescribable vistas that the traveler might wonder why villages were established on the mesas. They are not "pretty" or "photogenic," not like Mesa Verde, Canyon de Chelly, or Chaco Canyon. Yet, as with the Acoma mesa in New Mexico, people have lived and farmed here for hundreds of generations. Their physical and cultural persistence is in itself sufficient reason for respect, whether they came to the area in about 100 B.C. as science theorizes, or have in fact been here much longer. What is important is that the traveler appreciate both the extent and the depth of Hopi culture.

The three mesa communities are very close to one another, yet each speaks in its own dialect—plus another language of a "newcomer" population, the Tewa, who came to the Third Mesa only a couple of centuries ago.

In 1875, Major J.W. Powell visited and described life on the Three Mesas, and his account remains in print. Powell encountered the Hopi people almost immediately after a dangerous voyage down the Colorado River, and his account is filled with geographic and geologic descriptions of the Three Mesas area. He was guided by two rival missionaries, one a Methodist and the counterpoint a Mormon. The value of this small book to today's reader lies in its realism and introspection, in its wonderful illustrations, and in its identification of mesa communities such as Walpi, Sichum-na-Vi, Tewa, Shi-Mo-Pa-Vi, Oraibi, Mi-Shong-Na-Vi, and Shi-Paul-A-Vi, which still exist.

Travelers must cross many arid miles to reach the Three Mesas. In addition, one encounters mixed and confusing messages from maps and guidebooks. For example, some guidebooks say the village of Oraibi is "off-limits." But experience indicates that sometimes it is, and sometimes it is not. There are opportunities to park one's vehicle at the craft shop that is more or less the gateway to the town, then walk through certain neighborhoods accompanied by a guide. In virtually all cases, there are strict regulations against the taking of still or video pictures. Even making drawings or paintings of Hopi life is generally forbidden. On each mesa there is a museum, cultural center, bulletin board, or other source of information explaining Hopi rules and policies. Sad to say, there have been many insulting incidents, intentional or innocent, that have disrupted or embarrassed the Hopi people taking part in traditional ceremonies, dances, or just living their lives. As one woman said to a traveler, "It's not that *you* would not respect what we're doing, but there is the odd one who will not. So we must close everything and keep it to ourselves, at least for a while." We may not need a passport to enter a Native American nation, but we are there as visitors and guests in a sovereign country with its own rules and regulations.

Beautiful Hopi wicker baskets are bursting with color.

The sacred images of ceremonial dancers, called "kachinas," are representative of a living religion, one very complex in its seasonal and spiritual representation. There are hundreds of characters involved in the continuous calendar of life of the Hopi people. The multitude of these spiritually re-enacted and recreated spirits—good and bad—are part of Hopi daily life, not only relegated to celebrations. Kachinas in "doll-like" sculptures are sold at every tourist shop. These are not toys, but they were originally created for children, to help the youngsters understand sacred ceremonies and later participate in them.

If the traveler wants to learn more about kachinas or see more examples, there are books that explain them and museums that display them—like the Heard Museum in Phoenix, which has an amazingly extensive collection of kachinas loaned by Barry Goldwater, or the Museum of Northern Arizona in Flagstaff. On the Second Mesa, in Shungopavi, just west of the cultural center and museum, there is the Hopi Arts and Silvercrafts Co-operative Guild. If there are any fears kachina-buyers might feel buying from the multitude of stands that line highways or from coffee shop cases, a visit to the co-op can be enlightening. The visit will not only provide access to the multitude of different Hopi-made kachina spirit representations, but the Hopi salespeople there will also describe politely and enthusiastically what can be bought and what a kachina's significance is. The traveler can also take a small tour of the silversmithing guild's operation. Depending upon the day or the guide one can watch these special craftspeople create the Hopi designs on silver and copper for which they are known.

ABOVE: *This contemporary Hopi pot was created by Silvia Nahe, Hopi pueblo.*
RIGHT: *Kachinas, like this Hopi Ewiro kachina, are available at tourist shops and co-ops.*

How does one find the Three Mesas? If there is anything that distinguishes various reservations from the rest of the United States, it is the lack of all-weather and paved roads, signage, and places to ask for directions. There are about half-dozen entries to the Hopi Reservation, coming in from the four compass points. However, the recommended entry points are: northwest, via Tuba City (off U.S. 180 and AZ 264); from the south, via Winslow (I-40 north on AZ 87); or south from Holbrook (I-40 north on AZ 77 and Reservation 6); or coming in from Window Rock from the east on AZ 264. From the north it's a bit more difficult. Come off U.S. 160, which goes basically east-west from the Four Corners through the Navajo nation. Turn south on U.S. 191, passing Chinle—the entry point for the Canyon de Chelly National Monument—to the intersection of AZ 264, then turn right toward Tuba City.

The complexity of the directions indicates the isolation of the Hopi people. There are numerous on-reservation gravel dirt roads, but anyone wishing to travel these by-ways needs to stop at any of the tribal centers of Three Mesas to learn if there are any regulations. As one learns quickly in the Four Corners, there is not only the danger of getting lost or being a long way from any kind of services, there is also the possibility

Window Rock is a distinctive topographical formation.

that one might be traveling down a road to a site that is considered sanctified or holy.

Travelers must read their maps and realize that each time they enter a reservation, they are on "foreign" soil. The Navajo, the Hopi, the Apache, and the Zuni, unlike many of the other Native American nations, often do not tell the traveler when entrance has been gained to their land. The people who live there know where they are, always, and they are respectful of the borders and boundaries that non-Indians are not conscious of.

One way to tell when one has left Hopi country and has entered the Navajo nation is to look for the traditional Navajo hogan, which is a hexagonal or octagonal, single-storied dwelling. That traditional dwelling indicates that one is now on Navajo land.

We have chosen the Hopi as the first of the contemporary Native American peoples and nations that make the Four Corners area such a wonderful and complex blanket. If one comes to understand the sensitivity of the Hopi people, one will have less trouble traveling to other communities and reservations. One of the primary purposes of this book is to provide perspective into different cultures, thereby encouraging cautious, culturally aware interactions.

The Four Corners Monument gives travelers the chance to stand in four states at once.

ZUNI CULTURE

The Zuni nation is small in terms of space and population, yet the group's history is as profound as other Four Corner groups. It is impossible to consider the Native American experience in the Southwest and exclude the specificity of the Zuni. Those who study bloodlines or cultural linkages might believe that the Zuni descend from the Mogollon culture, while others insist they share the Hopi and Anasazi heritage.

Ashiwi is the word the Zuni people use to denote their heritage. It means "the flesh," or in broader terms "real folks," or "reality supporting our skeleton." The term "Zuni" derives from the river that flows through from the Colorado Plateau.

Why are these people different? The Zuni people are distinct from other Pueblo dwelling groups. They speak a different language, descended from the Penutian language family. Science indicates that the Zuni culture resulted from the prehistoric marriage of two groups, one from a northern region and the other from the south, possibly a part of the Mogollon peoples. Add to this mixture a very early merger with Mesoamericans who deserted Spanish expeditions and settled among the Zuni. Thus the Ashiwi people were formed.

Colorful regalia is part of Zuni festivals.

The Zuni are famous for special silver designs and patterns, as well as their kachina masks. The Museum of Northern Arizona in Flagstaff provides a dramatic demonstration of tribal differentiation. One might look at, for example, a turquoise and silver belt or necklace and see similarly exquisite artistry. Yet a closer examination reveals a vast difference in styles, use of materials, and the ultimate production.

Zuni, like the Hopi and the Navajo and some Pueblo people, continue the tradition of sacred kachina dolls and spiritual representations. Likewise, there are striking similarities in architectural design. Yet the Zuni built their pueblos of stone, not adobe, and then plastered the outer surface. Like the Sinaguan and Hohokam peoples, the Zuni adapted their constructions to the available building supplies.

When the Spanish arrived in the area, they noted the sequence of Zuni villages and called them the "Seven Cities of Cibola." Future fortune hunters would forget that "cibola" was the Spanish word for "buffalo," and would look for seven "lost" cities where the streets were paved in gold.

The relationship between the Zuni and the Spanish took a peculiar twist with the introduction in 1529 of the man who might be the first black man to enter the pages of North American history. Estavanico, known as "Estavan the Moor," lived for almost a decade with the various plains and southwestern tribes. Compared to the fair-skinned Spaniards, Estavan appeared so markedly different to the local people that he was revered. He charmed the Spanish with his tales of seven cities of gold and vast, unclaimed treasure.

However, his power was lost when he made contact with the Zuni. They killed him because he was impersonating a god and extorting sexual rights to Zuni women. His death halted the quest for the "Seven Cities of Cibola." Lose the messenger, lose his information. Some Spaniards called the Zuni response "arrogant," but Estavan had betrayed those who worshiped him.

According to Spanish history, Estavan's death did not discourage Fr. de Niza, a Spanish missionary, from moving northward. He went on to at least one more Zuni pueblo, Hawikuh, and later claimed this was the last stop on a very non-productive mission. What he added, though, was dangerous propaganda. He apparently misinterpreted the light at sunrise or sunset, mistaking its presence on the far cliffs for glistening gold begging to be excavated.

One year later, a Spanish explorer looked for that same vision.

Francisco de Coronado went in search of the seven cities, venturing as far as what is now Kansas. It was a most educational journey—far beyond previous European experience. The first military encounter with the Zuni did not bode well. There were no cities with streets of gold. There were no walls coated with precious jewels. Coronado had no riches when he died, and he never found the fabulous cities of gold.

The Arizona Zuni live on a small reservation between St. Johns and Holbrook, a few miles south of the Petrified Forest National Park. The reservation is almost impossible to reach, for there are no state or BIA roads into the area, which is more or less defined by two peaks—the North and South Mountains of the Stinking Creek range. The Zuni River flows through the reservation, joining the Little Colorado. Zuni tribal headquarters are located on the larger New Mexico reservation.

It is important to note that Arizona's own Native American Tourism Center, as well as numerous reference texts, do not refer to this small Zuni reservation as being open to the public for whatever reason.

A vista in the Painted Desert, located within the Petrified Forest National Park.

NAVAJO CULTURE

The Navajo, or Dineh, are the dominant Native American presence in the Four Corners. Not only do they have the largest tribal population in the entire country (1990 population approximately 250,000) but they also have the largest reservation in the U.S., about the same dimensions as West Virginia. The reservation covers about 16 million acres in Utah, Arizona, and New Mexico, but the largest portion is in Arizona.

In the middle of this huge reservation is the Hopi's allotted land. In the course of our description of the Navajo people—known to the Hopi as *Tasavuh*, a name that describes the Dineh's means of killing an enemy by crushing the skull with a stone axe—we will have to consider this relationship and coexistence, especially in light of recent court decisions regarding the distribution of land.

The Book of the Navajo by Raymond Locke is a very different kind of book than Frank Waters' *Book of the Hopi*. Locke is far more conventional in his historical approach, less dependent upon "native" narratives, and

Navajo girls in festive dress at Window Rock, Arizona.

includes more non-Navajo reports and histories. A scholar and student of Navajo/Dineh culture for decades, Locke nonetheless challenges a number of academic colleagues' theories or thoughts about why the Navajo and their fellow Athapascan-speaking Apache ended up in the Four Corners.

While there is still some question as to which group arrived first, most believe that the Apache arrived in about 825 A.D. and the Navajo in 1025 A.D. Others reverse the sequential emigration.

Dineh means, roughly "the people," and their land is "Dinehtah." It was the Pueblo who gave the Dineh the name "Navajo," a name that simply referred to a region where the Dineh lived.

Most contemporary anthropologists and archaeologists believe that the Navajo, like the Apache, came to the Four Corners from western Canada toward the end of the first millennium. However, the Navajo have their own interpretation of events and migrations.

There are many ways to interpret and recount history, but there is no question that the Navajo are a dominant culture in the Four Corners area. The Pueblo have their version of history, which describes how the Navajo and Apache occupied the Anasazi places in Chaco Canyon and Canyon de Chelly. Remember, too, that "Anasazi" is a Navajo word for "Old Enemies," while the Hopi and Pueblo have other words with dramatically different meanings to describe what they consider their ancestral linkages. These conflicts of historical interpretation and relationships will continue unresolved through the millennia.

Central to Navajo life is the hogan. In fact, in many places the presence of this unique structure is the only way a traveler can tell if he or she is on a Navajo reservation. There are male and female hogans, but the female, six-sided, single-story building is predominant today—the Navajo are a matriarchal society.

All hogans have some commonalities. The door always faces east. There is a hole in the middle of the roof that lets smoke escape from a fire that is always in the center of the dwelling. There are sweat hogans and simple shelter hogans; there are hogans built of forked sticks that look like a wooden "teepee" or an inverted "V."

For the Navajo, the hogan is more than a sweat lodge or a temporary place to get out of the wind, or even a home. The hogan is a sacred gift. Inside, there are places designated for the people's objects and activities. The south side, for example, is the women's place. The men have the north side. Visitors sit on the west side, facing the door. The richer the family, the more hogans there are within the compound.

Those people fortunate enough to be guests of a Navajo family will be led to the proper place, and depending upon the level of friendship, may be told what the directional differences are. If the traveler is fortunate enough to be invited into a hogan, it is best to allow oneself to be guided, and to be patient and respectful always, as is proper when a stranger enters someone's home.

Also, the honor of invitation belongs to the host, not the guest. So, to ask to enter any hogan is not only impolite but undiplomatic. There are many places where "model" hogans are constructed, and it is even possible to find Navajo craftspeople who replicate miniature hogans and sell them on the reservation or in some of the parks and monuments.

To appreciate the depth of the Navajo organization and tribal autonomy, though, we need to seek the roots of this special culture. Theirs is "The Land of the Rainbow." The Navajo sing and tell a multitude of songs and stories to their children, and these continue through adulthood.

The hogan is central to Navajo life.

Canyon de Chelly—another Spanish mispronunciation of Indian language—was called *Tsegi*, which simply meant "rock canyon." But in a traditional history called "Dine Bi Keyah," Tsegi is the center of the Navajo universe. Where Canyon de Chelly and Monument Canyon meet, even today, one is stunned by the great sandstone spikes that rise nearly 1,000 feet above sea level. This is the land of the Holy People.

Hozho is a Dineh word for "walking in beauty." It is a constant search for balance and spiritual equilibrium. One's life, one's health, and one's future all depend upon that delicate sense of harmony. When one loses "hozho," one becomes sick, ill, or in pain, inflictions that demand ceremonial redemption. This is the central factor of both natural and familial Navajo life. It also is extended into the creation of arts and crafts, of dance, of song and poetry. In many ways, hozho resembles the Zen concept of peace of mind through harmonic balance.

How does the non-Navajo discover the way of the "Rainbow of Life," where hozho began? The Hopi have their detailed description of the evolution of the "Peaceful People," and the Navajo have a different yet remarkably parallel series of passages describing how the people endured and encountered Creation.

The Navajo refer to their land as "The Land of the Rainbow."

According to the Navajo, there were once four worlds. Each world produced particular leaders or spiritual guides, finally numbering six. The Primary Creator, whose name reveals the matriarchal system that has sustained the Dineh-Navajo people from the beginning, can be translated to mean "The Love a Mother Gives Her Child." The various worlds are located in different mountain ranges of the Four Corners, and are now called the Sangre de Christos, the Jemez Range, and the further western Chuskai and Black Ranges. What is considered "The Navajo Place of Emergence," though, is found in the mountains of southern Colorado, very near today's Silverton—a historic mining town nestled in a convergence of valleys and surrounded by great peaks. What these various ranges create is a kind of frame, bounded by the San Francisco set of peaks near Flagstaff, the mountains of Colorado in the northern section, and the most sacred high points of New Mexico to the south and west.

It is impossible here to describe the approximately 800 songs that were sung by the Navajo elders when the Spanish first arrived. These are interpretations of the voices of the mountains and their spirits. The Navajo, the Hopi, and the Zuni all have ritual poetry that reflects the same colors, the same sacred directions, and the universal powers of life—air, earth, fire,

Full Moon Arch, in Mystery Valley, is found on the Navajo Reservation.

and water. The coincidence is not lost today, despite differences and antagonisms. Each had a "way," a "path," or a substantial means of guidance from one generation to the next, based always upon traditions.

Mountain ranges were significant, but so were particular geologic formations like those now called Window Rock, Shiprock, Chaco Canyon, Canyon de Chelly, and many others that were sculpted by time, water, and wind. These natural sculptures reflect the spirit of creation and the shaping of this earth. While travelers stand in awe of great, snow-covered ranges, there is no question that something special happens when one stands before an isolated rock formation and watches the sun and moon change the colors, shape, and dimension of the rocks. The Four Corners are filled with these "cathedrals." The modern traveler, aiming a camera at some marvelous shape within a series of horizons, may encounter the same feeling of inspiration that caused the Navajo, the Hopi, and the Zuni to pause and sing a reverent hymn.

The Navajo homeland is not much different in size than it has been for the past four centuries or so. However, the personality of the tribe has gone through major modifications. In the years before first contact with

Batakin Ruin is part of the Navajo National Monument in Tonalea.

the Europeans, in particular the Spanish, the Dineh were a bellicose people noted for their war-like attitude toward other tribal entities on the Colorado Plateau. Between the Navajo and the Apache, there was much to fear among the Pueblo descendants of the Mogollon and Anasazi.

However—and no one is certain why—the Navajo began to change their ways. They continued to demonstrate their militant strength, but they also began to adopt many of the agricultural styles of their neighbors. There is something to be said for the occasional periods of extreme drought that plague the Southwest. Just as the Sinaguan and Hopi, Zuni and other Pueblo peoples were able to cope with hard times through agricultural proficiency, so the Navajo turned to tilling the soil and domesticating certain crops. All these changes were gradual, subtly entering the mainstream of Navajo life, including their arts and crafts.

The cross-cultural transfer of methods took a quantum leap with the arrival of the Spanish and their European ways of doing things. The Spanish affected many tribes in the Four Corners area almost immediately. Their first known or documented contact with the Navajo was in 1626, almost a century after the first of the Spanish southwestern explorations.

This does not mean that the Navajo had not already grasped some of the improvements that could be incorporated into their way of living, such as the raising of sheep and goats plus some new crops. There was a wide-ranging trade network built over centuries between different nationalities. These linkages extended from Mezo-America to what is now Canada and as far west as the Great Lakes.

If there was one single import that changed the face and fate of Native Americans of the southwest and the Great Plains, it was the Spanish "gift" of the horse. The Navajos, the various southern groups, and the Pueblo Indians endured the many indignities of domination by the Spanish—soldiers, priests, slave traders, adventurers—for about 50 years.

Those familiar with early Spanish history in the Southwest cannot help but be stunned by the brutality of the invaders and by their enslavement, physically and spiritually, of the native peoples of the region. In 1680, however, a Tewa shaman or spiritual leader named Pope, pronounced "Po-pay," proclaimed that the Spanish domination must end. So, with great care and calculation, Pope engineered a most magnificent revolution, called "the Pueblo Rebellion" in history books.

Pope convinced peoples who lived in different places, spoke different languages, and had different heritages and lifestyles to rise up and push the

dominant colonial power from their land. It is an exciting story.

After meeting secretly with many tribal representatives, Pope sent runners from his San Juan pueblo across the countryside. They carried ropes made of maguey fibers; each rope indicated the number of days remaining before the war would commence.

On August 11, 1680, the many tribes, including the Peaceful People—the Hopi, in their only rebellious action against the Europeans—turned against soldiers, the Church and its priests and missionaries, the settlers or ranchers, the traders, and the governmental authorities. Many were killed, but Pope's vision was achieved. The Spanish all left the Arizona-New Mexico area, retreating to El Paso to lick their wounds and make plans to recover "their" lost territory.

The Spanish plotted their return for 12 years. Meanwhile, Pope became his own kind of dictator, demanding that all Indians reject all Spanish ways and return to their own.

It was a marvelous exercise in independence. Some tribes did totally reject all that was European, especially tools and religion. However, there were certain imports that could not be so easily dismissed—most importantly, the horse. The Navajo and the Hopi, even the Pueblo, soon became expert horse traders. And various Great Plains tribes almost immediately became their best customers.

Imagine for a moment what it was like for a people to hunt buffalo or herds of deer and antelope across vast open spaces. Anyone who has traveled the Great Plains always remarks at the infinite sea of grass and the endless horizon, even if traveling by car. Imagine people who traveled such distances on foot in order to preserve their small tribal and family units. Some would create grassfires to drive herds of buffalo over the rare cliff or arroyo, just to get enough food, hide, and bone to make it through the year.

The horse must have seemed to the Plains Indians a supreme gift, as it did indeed come to infiltrate their spiritual and tribal life. Horses could breed more horses. So, in the 1680s, the Navajo became very interested in the new trade commodity, as were the Apache.

The horse trading didn't stop when the Spanish came back in 1692, determined to fully dominate the native tribes. For more than a century, though, the Navajo and their Apache brothers refused to accept that European vision of historical progression. The athletic and elusive Apache kept to the mountain ranges and valleys they called home, while

Navajo sheperds lead their flock through the rugged landscape of Canyon de Chelly.

the more sedentary Navajo kept up a constant series of raids and acts of revenge upon all who invaded their territory.

When the Spanish, then the Mexican, authorities began their own kinds of retaliation, kidnapping youths and children for slaves, the Navajo retaliated by attacking Mexican settlements, repatriating slaves, capturing hostages, and taking herds of livestock. By 1846, when the U.S. government occupied New Mexico Territory, including Arizona, the raids and warfare had not ceased.

Military confrontation yielded treaties. But for nearly 20 years, these were tenuously followed by the more militant Indians. In 1860, Navajo Chief Manuelito and his comrade Baboncito attacked Fort Defiance, in what is now Arizona. They did not take the fort; instead, they were chased into the Chuska Range. During the American Civil War, the fighting continued. It was with the assignment of Col. Christopher "Kit" Carson in 1862, that things turned dramatically against the Navajo and the Apache. Carson followed Sherman's theory of cutting a destructive

This model created by Tom Parquette shows a Navajo eagle dancer.

swath across the entire territory, attacking not only the people but their communities and all that sustained them.

In January of 1864, Carson took his troops into both ends of Canyon de Chelly. The Navajo were trapped inside, and the "resistance" was broken. Two months later, 6,000 homeless, half-starved Navajo surrendered. By December, another 2,000 had come in from the cold. The Navajo who surrendered in 1864 faced "The Long Walk," which stretched for 300 miles from Fort Defiance to Fort Sumner, south of Sante Fe.

In 1866, 4,000 remaining Navajo capitulated, including Manuelito. They, too, would make the terrible trek to Fort Sumner. Not only were they humiliated by removal from their homelands, but they were isolated in the middle of nowhere familiar. About 200 died during "The Long Walk." Eventually, some 2,000 would perish in captivity.

In 1868, a bizarre reversal of U.S. policy occurred: Let the people go home. Let them fend for themselves. Supporting so many people was a drain on a hard-pressed, post-Civil War government. Many, old and young, died on the way *back* to their land. It's estimated that one-fourth of the Navajo people died during this period.

Every Navajo today knows about "The Long Walk." The genealogy of every family was affected, and all families lost home, land, and the freedom to be.

Despite such tragedies, the Dineh people, the Navajo, have proven the resilience of their culture and way of life. Fewer and fewer people speak Navajo as their primary language, but many are bilingual or even trilingual, so the traveler can yet encounter Navajo traditions, history, and culture throughout the Southwest.

APACHE CULTURE

The name "Apache" is a Zuni word for "enemy." Apache people speak Athapascan language, in the same family as the Navajo. However, while there is only one Dineh culture, there are a dozen or so Apache groups, mostly dictated by the territory they held and defended. Generally, it is thought that the Apache arrived in the region around 1300 A.D.

First an index of Apache peoples: In Arizona, there are the bands of the San Carlos, Aravaipa, White Mountain, Northern Tonto, Southern Tonto, and Cibecue; the Chiracahua and Mimbreno live here and in New Mexico. The Jicarilla live in New Mexico and Colorado; the Mescalero live in New Mexico and Mexico; the Lipan live in Texas; the Kiowa-Apache have land in Oklahoma.

Each Apache band within the nation has its own historical and cultural differences. While we know the tribal name as a generic one, their traditions, their relations with non-Apaches, and their history of defensive encounters almost always resulted from the autonomous decisions of each group.

While they were largely nomadic hunters of regional game and gatherers of natural vegetation, the Apache also became efficient and effective raiders of Pueblo villages and later Spanish, Mexican, and Anglo-American settlements. In some cases, such as with the Apache in eastern Arizona, contact with the Pueblos also led them to become farmers themselves. To the east, because of contact with the Plains Indians, they pursued the great buffalo herds as well. In the "deep" southwest, the Lipan Apache took on many of the sustaining characteristics of the Mexican tribes nearby.

Instead of hogans, the Apache lived in wickiups, pole-framed domes covered with reed mats or grass and brush. Some adopted the Plains Indians' tipi-style structure. As hunters, they wore animal-skin garments. They did not make pottery or do much weaving, but they were exceptional basket makers. Interestingly, after the arrival of the Europeans, they created a single-string "Apache fiddle," which was made from a yucca stalk and played with a sinew-strung bow.

The Apache, while governed in small units by a singular headman, shared a spiritual heritage that recognized supernatural beings such as "Yusan," the Giver of Life and the strongest of all powers. Shamans, or holy men, conducted rituals important to their existence. The Mountain Spirits, or "Gans," were represented in human form by dancers wearing

kilt-like apparel and masks of black that had headdresses made of wooden strips. Body paint was an important element in these ritual dances.

For centuries, the Apache fought every invader and seemed invincible. Only the Plains Comanche proved stronger when they emigrated south in the mid-1700s. The struggle for territory continued through the 1860s. At that time the names of Apache leaders became part of Western history. Cochise, Mangas Colorado, and Eskiminzin were among the most militant. Each in turn was defeated by the more powerful U.S. forces. Treaties were strictly enforced, and President Ulysses S. Grant demanded that reservations for the Apache be established.

The Apache and the Yavapai disputed resettlement, and the Apache Wars continued. New leaders emerged in the 1870s, including Victorio, a Mimbreno Apache, and Geronimo, a Chiricahua. Both led uprisings on Arizona's San Carlos Reservation. Although captured, they escaped into the mountains and kept fighting. Victorio's Rebellion lasted three years until he was finally defeated by the Mexican army and killed.

Geronimo's Rebellion lasted from 1881 until 1886. It was the last extended refusal to obey the directives and treaties of the U.S. government. Geronimo and his valiant struggle are very much a part of the history of Arizona and the Southwest. General Nelson Miles sent 5,000

The Apache are traditionally known for thier exceptional basketry.

troops and cavalrymen into the field to stop a small band of Apache led by Geronimo. Time, supplies, age, and numbers finally made him capitulate in Skeleton Canyon, close to Apache Pass in Arizona. It was very near the place where the Apache Wars had begun a quarter-century earlier.

Geronimo's end rivals that of many whose names are noted in American Indian history. In chains, along with a number of his warriors, Geronimo was sent to Fort Pickens in Pensacola, Florida, after being imprisoned for a time in Alabama. He watched his fellow Apaches slowly die of disease, dislocation, and depression. There was some public protest, for Geronimo had achieved national prestige, so these Apaches were ultimately sent back to the west. But not to their homeland. Arizona refused to allow Geronimo and his band to return, so he was shunted to Oklahoma. A prisoner of war, he died at Fort Sill on the Comanche and Kiowa Reservation in 1909. Those Chiricahua who survived were finally allowed to return home five years later.

The San Carlos Reservation remains in existence today, located in Gila and Graham counties of Arizona. The Apache also share a small piece of land with the Yavapai on a reservation near Camp Verde. There are many Apache reservations, shared and separate, throughout Arizona.

Tonto National Monument reveals an amicable merging of cultures, as Apache predecessors learned from the resident Hohokam how to use the Tonto Creek, as it flows into Salt River. The "marriage" of energies and inventiveness created wonderful pottery, marvelous fabrics, and colors or dyes found nowhere else in the Southwest. This happened between 1100 and 1300, it is estimated. In the 14th century some people decided to build cliff dwellings of rock, clay and adobe mortar. These builders then applied a smooth surface plaster to the exteriors. For a mere half-century, folks occupied these homes, and then, again as with so many, they were abandoned. Today the ruins of these 600-year old dwellings may be visited. The National Monument has a visitor's center where displays and books describe the lives of the people of the lower Tonto Creek.

PAIS CULTURE

Long ago, in what is now northwestern Arizona, there were people the anthropologists and archaeologists call Patayan or Hakataya. Their livelihood was based upon the flowage of the Colorado River south of the Grand Canyon. They were hunters, but they also used seasonal floods to irrigate areas where crops could grow. Some consider them the "fourth" branch, kin of the Mogollon, the Anasazi, and the Hohokam, especially the latter in their earliest "pioneer" development.

Today the traveler will find three basic "Upland Yuman-speaking" Pai groups: The Hualapai, the Havasupai, and the Yavapai. The separation comes, again, with language, for the Mohave and the Yuma speak what is called "River Yuman" language. So, somewhere along the line the Patavan or Hakataya branched off according to dialect and then language.

THE HUALAPAI

Sometimes called *Walapai*, meaning the "Pine Tree People," the Hualapai might be an appropriate introduction to the Pai culture—in part because the reservation town of Peach Springs (on old U.S. 66) affords the traveler access to the bottom of the Grand Canyon by four-wheel-drive. Peach Springs is also the only place where one can obtain official permits to hunt, fish, and travel the canyon that is the reservation's rambling northern boundary. This is important not only for traveling, but because the reservation includes the lower 100 miles of the continent's greatest canyon.

The Hualapai claimed the territory between what belonged to the Mohave and the Havasupai. While the region might be considered one of the most spectacular geological formations in the world, people cannot eat scenery or the horizon, or drink only from the muddy Colorado River. Therefore, the Hualapai lived a relatively simple life of seasonal migrations, eating available roots and herbs, and planting on a random flood plain that depended upon snowmelt and rainfall far to the north.

The people lived in huts built from shrubs, bushes, and driftwood, and they fished and hunted whatever was available. Their clothing was made of skins or bark fibers. In the winters, they wore robes of fur-bearing animals they had killed.

The Hualapai's culture was not one of sophisticated songs and poems. Although the Spanish undoubtedly made early contact with the Hualapai, no one paid much attention to them until about the time of the American

Revolution, when Spanish missionaries and explorers began passing more regularly through the area. One hundred years later, the U.S. government officially established the Hualapai Reservation.

THE HAVASUPAI

Around 1100 A.D., a group of Pai people settled along an area east of what is now the Hualapai Reservation. These are the Havasupai, and their homeland is also along the edge of the Grand Canyon, although not on the Colorado River. Some think that the Havasupai—literally, "People of the Blue-Green Water"—were so named because they lived in the area of what is called Cataract Canyon. This proved to be a small and fertile space with abundant water, unlike the territory inhabited by their neighbors.

The Havasupai became eager and productive farmers, growing melons, squash, corn, beans, sunflowers, and the universal spiritual crop—tobacco. There was no need for the Havasupai to move from this productive place. They possessed the agricultural currency to negotiate with almost all groups in the Southwest. They recognized their own prosperity with their architecture, for they built pole-frame dwellings and rock buildings. They also had domed buildings that were both sweat lodges and meeting rooms.

Somehow, the Hopi had more to do with the Havasupai than other Pai cultures, so there is much residual history shared, both spiritually and culturally. While the Hualapai remained relatively "rural" because of the scarcity of their own resources, the Havasupai were ideal trading partners, for they not only had things like skins and paint-substances, they also had salt. In many ways it was their access and processing of that special "Colorado" color, a ruddy pigment used in dyes and paints, that made trade worthwhile. The Havasupai also extended the art of buckskin apparel, the use of body paint, and the introduction of facial tattooing.

For the Havasupai, the family was and still is the central unit of all being. Their six chiefs ascended through familial groups. Priests or shamans preside over a tradition of three annual ceremonies. These feature music, dancing, and the art of speechmaking or storytelling.

Supai, Arizona, is now home to the Havasupai, on a reservation established in 1880. The reservation is located a half-mile below the southern rim of the Grand Canyon. The Havasupai are noted for their basketry and beadwork, but one must understand that Supai is not easy to reach. In fact, the road ends some eight miles from the village, and one must proceed on foot or on horseback.

THE YAVAPAI

Of all the Pai peoples, the Yavapai ranged the farthest. While the Havasupai and the Hualapai were apparently content to stay in their homelands along the Colorado River, the Yavapai migrated throughout north-central and even central Arizona. The lifestyle of the Yavapai, whose language is a dialect of the Yuman language family, was in many ways closely related to that of the Apache. In some references, they are even called the "Mohave Apache" or the "Yuma Apache." The Yavapai divided themselves into three main groups: the Kawevikopaya in the southeastern region of Arizona; the Yawepe in the northeast; and the Tolkepaya in the western portion of what is now Arizona.

Like their northern kin, the Hualapai, the Yavapai were not noted for their farming. Instead, they depended upon the natural harvest of wild desert and canyon vegetation. Those who spent time near the Mojave people learned to grow corn and other staples, including tobacco, but these were a minority. All groups included hunters, and the Yavapai's domed, brush-covered houses, along with their use of cave dwellings, are reminiscent of the Apache. Like the Apache, the Yavapai fought vehemently against the Spanish and Mexican forces, and staunchly resisted attempts at religious conversion.

Together with the Tonto Apaches, the Yavapai rebelled against the U.S. Army in a fight that was essentially lost in 1872. General George Crook's cavalry at that time pursued what was called the "Tonto Basin Campaign." At the Battle of Skull Cave, many Yavapai and Apache warriors were killed by ricocheting bullets and by an avalanche created by the soldiers. The Yavapai resistance crumbled, and survivors and their families were sent to reservations at Camp Verde (north of Phoenix), or to the San Carlos Reservation. Eventually, Yavapai and Apaches were also sent to the Fort McDowell Reservation.

The traveler will not find much to see at either McDowell or Camp Verde. The Fort McDowell Reservation is headquartered in Needles, California, and is a destination mainly for those seeking to gamble at the reservation casino. Camp Verde Reservation is a tiny portion of a small town of the same name, derived from the historic presence of Fort Verde. According to the local chamber of commerce and the local historical society, the area contains America's most complete reconstructed military encampment. Of the two, Camp Verde has more to offer the traveler, including the nearby sites of Montezuma Castle and Montezuma Well. It

Apache dancers at White River, Arizona.

is also situated near Sedona and the glorious red-rock formations of Oak Creek Canyon. The reservation owns the largest motel in the area and two fine gift shops, but when one considers that the Yavapai and their Apache neighbors once claimed much of the region as their homeland, it seems a modest estate.

This displacement is, of course, one of the great tragedies the traveler encounters throughout North America; everywhere, cultures that were once dominant and fought to keep their homelands were forcibly moved into what seem vastly inferior territories.

By taking a brief swing through Camp Verde off Highway 17, at the first exit proceeding north from Phoenix, the traveler will see the standard H.U.D. dwellings set along the creek. These provide ample testimony of the Yavapai culture's change of stature as time has passed. Heading toward Montezuma Castle, there is evidence of rich farm and ranch country which, of course, brought the U.S. Army to the area. The army built Fort Verde as a mighty signal of their intention to protect the American settler.

PIMA CULTURE

The Gila River Reservation, located only 40 miles south of Phoenix, is considered the home of the Pima people. "Pima" is a misunderstood response to questions posed by early Spanish explorers. The response, "pi-nyi-match," meant simply "I don't know," but the Spanish interpreted it as a self-description.

The people's real name is *Ah-kee-mult-o-o-tam*, or "River People," a name describing their homeland. The name distinguishes them from their neighbors, who also spoke the Uto-Aztecan language, who were called the *Tohono O'odham* or "Desert People." Remember, those called the Hohokam, a Pima word for "the Vanished Ones," are considered by many to be the Pima's antecedents. However, there is some evidence that the presence of the Pima and Tohono O'odham populations might have caused the Hohokam to "vanish" or move north.

The Pima have always been an agricultural people, as well as hunters and fishers. Living along the Gila and Salt rivers, they built small, round, pole-framed dwellings, square huts for storage, and open "ramadas" (lean-tos) for protection against the elements. Corn, cotton, squash, beans, tobacco, and later alfalfa and wheat were grown. Wild fruits and vegetables were gathered. Cotton was a key to the culture, for it was woven into clothing, and willow wands were used to make baskets. The composition of the local soil enabled the women to create a highly-polished pottery colored in black and red. Bark and other fibers, as well as animal skins, were used to make additional clothing and blankets.

There was a chief for the entire tribe, as well as village chieftains. Each place also had a ceremonial leader, the "Keeper of the Smoke." The villages were organized into two clans, the Red Ant Clan and the White Ant Clan. In their spiritual hierarchy, "Earthmaker" and "Elder Brother" were the most powerful presences.

The Pima were often harassed by the Apache, but they held their ground. Yet when the Spanish arrived in the late 16th century, the Pima offered little opposition at the start, perhaps because the Spanish also introduced the people to new crops and livestock. Violence occurred when the Spanish began to exact taxes from the Pima. In 1695, they rebelled, were repelled, and retreated north to join relatives. There was another rebellion in 1751, caused mainly by the Spanish forcing Pima into slavery. One leader organized the Tohono O'odham, the Apache, and a small group called the Sobaipuris in a rebellion. They destroyed many Spanish missions and ranches.

The U.S. government entered the scene in 1853, following the Gadsden Purchase of land from Mexico. The acquisition of land lured a number of non-Indian, Anglo-American settlers, who proceeded to seize Pima land for their own use and divert the Pima water resources onto their own lands. The Gila River Reservation was established in 1859, but two decades later the Pima were relocated to the land where they now live, and a "new" reservation was created.

Today the Pima share the Gila River Reservation with the Maricopa people, who had fled to this area after they were attacked by the Yuma tribe.

TOHONO O'ODHAM CULTURE

Arizona's second-largest reservation is located 70 miles south of Phoenix. It's identified on older maps as the Papago Reservation, but considered by the people as the Tohono O'odham Reservation. The people were called "Papago" by the Pima, a name meaning "the Bean People," but they prefer their own description of "the Desert People."

Related to the Uto-Aztecan language group, the Tohono O'odham lived where little water flowed, and where hunting and gathering were the means of subsistence. They were dependent upon the beneficence of the natural world, including the rare resource provided by rainfall. At some times, they were "hired" by the Pima to help harvest their crops, and they were paid in the form of food.

The group's contact with the Spanish, Mexican, and American authorities parallel the Pima experience. In the 1860s, a series of Apache raids threatened the people of the Gila River and lower Salt River region, so the Tohono O'odham joined forces not only with the Pima and the Maricopa, but also with the Anglos living in the area. Eventually, the Tohono O'odham were able to establish three homelands in Arizona Territory, including the one headquartered in Sells. Their other homelands are the Ak-Chin Reservation, shared with the Maricopa, and the San Xavier Reservation south of Tucson.

MOJAVE CULTURE

Travelers, truck drivers, tourists—all outsiders know the fabled Mohave Desert (also spelled "Mojave"), but few know of the Mohave nation. Their tribal name comes from *Aha-makave*, which generally means "Beside the Water." Between the desert and the Mojave and Colorado rivers, there has long lived a group of people of Yuman-speaking heritage. The Upland Yumans are the Havasupais, the Hualapais, and the Yavapais. Despite the Mojave people's proximity to California's border and the "Great Basin," theirs is still considered a Southwestern nation, although the Mojave are among the farthest residents of the neighborhood.

Their kinship with the Upland Yumans is a reason for their inclusion in this book. Their homeland's western border was one of the continent's harshest deserts, but all the while they managed to live along the shores of flowing waters. Spring floods provided natural irrigation, the river provided fish and watering sites for game—both fowl and four-leggeds. They, like so many others, used the pinon nuts and mesquite beans as staple vegetables, supplemented by plentiful desert fruits and roots. Their habitat defined their habits and their dwellings. They built homes that were cool in the summer and moved to warmer homes in the winter. They wore cotton garments in the warm weather and skins in the winter.

The Mojave were renowned for their ferocity when threatened by either hostile natural elements or people who attempted to invade their territory. They did not have peaceful relations with the Pima or Tohono O'odham who roamed in search of resources to sustain their own peoples. At the same time, the Mojave's special place on the great Colorado River allowed them to take advantage of the natural north-south trade route. They became raft-builders and skilled aquatic navigators, unlike most southwestern groups.

Spanish contact took place in the 16th century, but the quest was for souls to save rather than the Seven Cities of Gold. The Mojave rejected missionary adventurers. By 1775, though, the Mojave people agreed to work as guides for the Spanish up the Colorado River's Grand Canyon. The Spanish did not like the Mojave, for they refused to conform to colonial demands unless they stood to gain from acquiescence. They continued their raids upon European travelers, settlements, and migrations even after the California Gold Rush of 1848-49. When the U.S. built Fort Yuma at the Yuma Crossing of the river following the Mexican Cession of 1848, the Mojave violence decreased.

Today there are three Mojave reservations. There is the Fort Yuma Reservation headquartered in Yuma (about 190 miles from Phoenix); the Fort Mojave Reservation, headquartered in Needles, California (about 250 miles from Phoenix); and the Colorado River Reservation, headquartered in Parker, Arizona.

CONCLUSION

A number of smaller tribal nationalities exist in Arizona, including the Yaqui, the Cocopah, the Kaibab-Paiute. We were not able to discuss all of them, but the groups listed in this chapter reveal the variety and concentration of Native American populations and locations in present-day Arizona.

The term "conclusion" really does not apply to Native American life in Arizona, or to the accessibility of the multitude of national cultures that continue to exist there today. As we have noted, the tribal boundaries do not exactly follow the state's dimensions.

The history of the many peoples who resided in this region long before European incursions, far exceeds our descriptions. Their own historic and spiritual connections to what we now call Arizona make the Spanish and Anglo contribution to southwestern life seem minimal. Yet the new residents sought dominance, and quickly succeeded in oppressing native populations.

That dominance, however, in no way diminishes the profound heritage of the Native Americans who still consider their homelands sacred. Travelers visiting any of these cultures need to be mindful and respectful of these long histories.

Even more important, though, is the fact that there are many sites and locations in Arizona which extend beyond the various reservation boundaries. It is worthy to note that it's illegal to deface or steal from a ruin even if it is not within official boundaries. Even casual gathering of "souvenirs" may be offensive, illegal, and sacrilegious.

The simple sign at Tuzigoot National Monument lays down the traveler's code most succinctly: "Take only photographs. Leave only footprints on the paths."

This is not meant as a warning but as a word to the wise. The traveler, the tourist, the non-Arizona Indian—all have the responsibility to leave everything in place. Much has already been disturbed by scientists, even in reconstructing a wonderful place like Tuzigoot, all done in the name of "understanding," "archaeology," or "tourism." In many cases, even the scientists did not know what was being violated.

There are dimensions to the spiritual life of the Native American that most non-Indians do not comprehend. To disturb or desecrate a sacred place is to send the souls of the people into oblivion, where they may wander aimlessly and have no purpose beyond their earthly lives. On the other hand, to visit respectfully all native places and people is to honor them and their remarkable heritage.

MUSEUMS, ARCHIVES, AND CULTURAL CENTERS

Amerind Foundation, Inc. (P.O. Box 248, Dragoon 85609) houses one of the finest collections of prehistoric and historic Indian artifacts in the world. The private museum contains an extensive collection of prehistoric material from the area once called Pimeria Alta, which included southern Arizona and the northern part of the Mexican state of Sonora. It is open by appointment only on Saturdays and Sundays year-round. Admission is free. From Tucson drive 64 miles east on Interstate 10, then one and a quarter miles on the local road toward Dragoon.

Arizona State Museum at the University of Arizona (N. Park Ave. at University Blvd., Tucson 85721) features exhibits of all major cultures in Southwest prehistory, including artifacts form Ventana Cave, Snaketown, and the Naco and Lehner sites. Open Monday through Saturday afternoons; admission is free.

Arizona State University Museum of Anthropology (anthropology building, Arizona State University, Tempe) contains exhibits designed and installed by university students, displaying a variety of material from the collection of the anthropology department as well as other institutions. A number of displays emphasize archaeological techniques for studying artifacts and the material culture of prehistoric people. Also included are exhibits on dental anthropology, showing how the teeth of ancient Americans reveal the areas in Asia where their groups probably originated. Open Monday through Friday; admission is free.

Canyon De Chelly Museum (P.O. Box 588, Chinle 86503) exhibits archaeological finds from the Four Corners area and artifacts from later Navajo culture. From Gallup, New Mexico, drive north 8 miles on U.S. 666, then 52 miles west on New Mexico-Arizona 264 through Ganado, then 33 miles north on Navajo 63 to the monument, headquarters and visitor center at Chinle.

Casa Grande Ruins Museum (1100 Ruins Dr., P.O. Box 518, Coolidge 85228), located halfway between Phoenix and Tucson, features artifacts of the Hohokam people and panels explaining their lives. Located about a mile north of Coolidge off U.S. Interstate 10, the museum is accessible via the exit for Arizona Highway 387. There is a town on U.S. 10 called Casa Grande, but it is not part of the historic site.

Navajo jewelry is displayed at many museums.

Casa Malpais Museum (318 Main St., Springerville 85938; 602-333-5375) features excavated artifacts from the Casa Malpais ruins and conducts tours of the site.

Clara T. Woody Museum of the Gila County Historical Society (Box 2891, 1330 N. Broad, Globe 85502) exhibits artifacts from the ruins of a large village at a site called Besh-Ba-Gowah, which was inhabited from approximately 1225 to 1400 A.D. by the Salado people. From the center of Globe, take U.S. 60 west to the Mine Rescue Building at the north end of city. Open Monday through Friday afternoon; admission is free.

Colorado River Indian Tribes Museum (Rt. 1, Parker 85344) features exhibits that include Mohave, Chemehuevi, Navajo, and Hopi artifacts. The museum also features Anasazi, Hohokam, and Patayan collections. Open daily; admission is free.

Degrazia Art & Cultural Foundation (6300 N. Swan Rd., Tucson 85718) displays works by the late southwestern artist Ted Degrazia, in addition to works by local artists.

Eastern Arizona Museum and Historical Society (Main and Center Sts., Pima) displays Salado and Hohokam artifacts. Open Monday through Friday; admission is free.

Gila River Arts and Crafts Center (30 miles southeast of Phoenix, off I-10 at exit 175) is a multi-tribal arts center and cultural heritage park. Artifacts are on display and craft demonstrations and performances are held on weekends. Open daily, 9 am to 5 pm. Admission is free.

Heard Museum of Anthropology and Primitive Art (22 E. Monte Vista Rd., Phoenix 85004) offers collections built around artifacts of Indians of the Americas, including the Hohokam of southern Arizona. Open Tuesday through Saturday; admission is charged.

Mohave Museum of History and Arts (400 W. Beale, Kingman 86401) offers a miniature rendition of a typical Mohave Indian village, and displays Walapai, Mohave, and prehistoric pottery.

Museum of Anthropology at Eastern Arizona College (626 Church St., Thatcher 85552) displays artifacts from Mogollon, Anasazi and Hohokam material culture.

Museum of Northern Arizona (3001 N. Fort Valley Rd., Rt. 4, Box 720, Flagstaff 86001) is the first place to visit if you're looking for a learning experience that will help you distinguish the basic jewelry or weaving styles of the Colorado Plateau Indians—namely the Hopi, the Zuni, and the Navajo. The museum has three annual events: The Zuni show in late

May; the Hopi show from late June through the 4th of July; and the Navajo show in late July and early August. The museum also has exhibits covering all periods from the Paleo-Indian, Anasazi and Pueblo, through present-day Hopi and Navajo cultures. Open afternoons Monday through Saturday; admission is free.

Navajo Tribal Museum (Navajo Arts and Crafts Enterprise Building on Arizona 264, Window Rock) includes both Navajo artifacts and prehistoric Anasazi artifacts in its exhibits. Open Monday through Friday, October through April; Monday through Saturday, May through September. Admission is free. Group tours available.

Pueblo Grande Museum and Cultural Park (4619 East Washington Street, Phoenix 85034; 602-435-0900) is the only National Historic Landmark in the city. The large museum and archaeological site demonstrate the life of the Hohokam from approximately 300 B.C. to 1400 A.D. There are audio-visual narrations regarding the place and its long history; there is a walk-through exhibit; and there is a chance to take a relatively brief walk around a well-designed, respectfully preserved archaeological site. Open Monday through Saturday afternoons; admission is free.

Sharlot Hall (415 West Gurley, Prescott 86301) has a room devoted to prehistoric cultural material from Arizona, particularly from the area surrounding Prescott. Open Tuesday through Saturday afternoons; admission is free.

Smoki Museum (100 North Arizona, Box 123, Prescott 86301) is a smallish museum featuring a display of prehistoric Arizona artifacts gathered by a group of non-Indians calling themselves the Smoki. Open Tuesday through Saturday; admission is free.

Stradling Museum of the Horse (P.O. Box 413, Patagonia 85624) features equine and Indian exhibits.

Tonto National Museum (P.O. Box 707, Roosevelt 85545), allows visitors to follow a trail to cliff dwellings in which people lived nearly 600 years ago. The museum's exhibits include drawings, artifacts, and samples of Salado weaving, weapons, tools, and jewelry. From Globe, drive 4 miles west on U.S. 60; 28 miles northwest on Arizona 88 to the monument entrance; then one mile to the visitor's center. Open daily. Admission is charged. Group tours available.

Tuzigoot National Museum (P.O. Box 68, Clarkdale 86324) displays artifacts that were recovered during the excavation of the site. One exhibit shows burial practices in which adults were placed in holes scooped from the village trash heaps. From Flagstaff, drive 49 miles southwest on U.S. 89A to Cottonwood, then 3 miles northwest to the museum entrance. Open daily. Admission is charged.

Tucson Museum of Art (140 N. Main, Tucson 85701) displays treasures of Latin American, Pre-Columbian, and American art, as well as the work of southwestern and western artists.

Western Archaeological and Conservation Center (1415 N. Sixth Ave., Tucson 85717) displays southwestern prehistoric artifacts.

Wupatki National Museum (HC 33, Box 444A, Flagstaff 86001) features exhibits that demonstrate the tool and object-making skills of prehistoric Indians. From Flagstaff drive 32 miles north on U.S. 89 to the Wupatki-Sunset Crater Loop Rd. entrance, then 14 miles east to the visitor's center. Open year round; admission is free.

Yavapai Museum (Grand Canyon National Park, P. O. Box 129, Grand Canyon 86023) is a national historic landmark that features artifacts from the Tusayan prehistoric ruins.

MONUMENTS, HISTORIC SITES, AND PARKS

Ak-Chin Indian Community (Route 2, Box 27, Maricopa 85239; 602-568-2227) includes an Eco-Museum, a motel in Maricopa, and some of the Southwest's best views of the Sonoran Desert. San Xavier has as its centerpiece for travelers the San Xavier Del Bac Mission, and it is suggested that visitors contact the Native American Tourism Center in Phoenix (602-945-0771).

Canyon De Chelly National Monument (P.O. Box 588, Chinle 86503) allows visitors to walk to a cliff dwelling called White House Ruin, following trails that wind down from the canyon rim for over a mile. Open daily, year round; admission is free.

Casa Grande Ruins National Monument offers an excellent introduction to the life of the ancient irrigation farmers now known as the Hohokam. Open daily, all year. Admission is charged. Camping available nearby.

Casa Malpais (318 E. Main St., Springerville 85938; 602-333-5375) features the ruins of a Mogollon village believed to be a major trade and ceremonial center between 1265 and 1380 A.D. Tours leave from the Casa Malpais Museum.

Chiricahua National Monument (Dos Cabezas Rd., Box 6500, Willcox 85643) was the site of prehistoric volcanic eruptions, and is nicknamed the Wonderland of Erosion. It is located off I-10 south of

Willcox, near Apache Pass.

Cochise Stronghold (P.O. Box 308, Pearce 85625), located south of Interstate 10 near Benson, is a natural fortress in the east face of the Dragoon Mountains, where Cochise sought refuge from the U.S. Cavalry after a raid during the Indian wars.

Fort Bowie National Historic Site (south of I-10 near Wilcox) commemorates the fort, established in 1862, that protected the Butterfield Trail route known as the Apache Pass. Ruins of the fort still exist, but seeing them requires a one-and-a-half mile hike and a drive up dirt roads.

Fort McDowell Reservation, Mohave-Apache Tribal Council (500 Merriman Avenue, Needles, CA 92363; 619-326-4591) is about 35 miles northeast of Phoenix. What makes this a tourism destination, quite simply, is the Council's casino at the reservation's only town, Fort McDowell. Only a few paved highways cross or provide access to the reservation. Off-road travel on the reservation nearly always requires not only caution but permits from the tribal government. However, U.S. 60, AZ 73, AZ 260, and AZ 273, as well as BIA 8 provide access to some of the most scenic canyons, peaks, and valleys in Arizona.

Fort Verde State Historic Park, (off I-17 near the center of the town of Camp Verde) is a ten-acre park commemorating the U.S. Army garrison stationed there in the 1870s. Several of the fort's original buildings remain. The center displays military artifacts and relics left by Indians and settlers.

Ira Hayes Memorial and Library (Gila River Indian Community, P.O. Box 97, Sacaton 85247; 602-963-4323) commemorates Ira Hayes, a Pima Indian and perhaps the most famous of Native Americans serving in WWII. Hayes was one of six U.S. Marines who raised the American flag on Iwo Jima. He died in tragic obscurity in 1955, but his people have not forgotten his role as a valiant warrior in a place far from home.

Kinishba Pueblo can be reached by driving 15 miles west of Whiteriver on Arizona 73. A partly restored Mogollon-Anasazi pueblo, it housed a thousand or more people between A.D. 1100 and 1350. It is one of the largest ruins in the Southwest. Open year round; admission is free.

Kinlichee Tribal Park features preserved ruins of Anasazi dwellings, the oldest of which is a pithouse dated at approximately 800 A.D. From the Navajo Indian Reservation, drive 22 miles west from Window Rock on Navajo 3 (Arizona 264) to Cross Canyon Trading Post, then two-and-a-half miles north on a gravel road to Kinlichee and Cross Canyon Ruins.

Open year round; admission is free. Camping is available nearby.

Meteor Crater (40 miles east of Flagstaff, south off I-40) is the best-preserved meteor impact site on Earth. The crater is 570 feet deep and nearly three miles in circumference.

Mission San Xavier Del Bac (nine miles southwest of Tucson on Rt. 11) is the site of the Spanish Colonial Indian Mission of 1783.

Montezuma Castle National Monument (P.O. Box 219, Camp Verde 86332) is actually in two sections—Montezuma Castle and Montezuma Well, nine-and-a-half miles apart. From Flagstaff drive 50 miles south on Interstate 17, then two-and-a-half miles east to the visitor's center. Open daily, all year; admission is charged.

Monument Valley Tribal Park offers guided, four-wheel-drive trips to prehistoric ruins in the Monument Valley area. These can be arranged through the visitor's center. From Kayenta, drive 24 miles north on U.S. 163 to directional sign, then five miles east on the local road to the visitor's center. Open daily, June through September; admission is free.

The magnificent San Xavier Del Bac Mission is located nine miles southwest of Tucson.

Navajo National Monument (HC-71, Box 3, Tonalea 86044) features several superb cliff dwellings. These ancient villages were occupied 700 years ago by members of the prehistoric Kayenta Anasazi culture. One village has 135 rooms, built in an immense cave that reaches 500 feet in height. From Tuba City, drive 56 miles northeast on U.S. 160, then nine miles northwest on a paved road to the visitor's center. Open daily, year round; admission is free. Campsites are available.

Painted Desert (Interstate 40 east of Holbrook) is situated near the northern end of the Petrified Forest National Park. The area earned its name from its magnificent purple, red, and gray sediments, which form moonscape mounds.

Painted Rocks State Park contains a group of Indian rock art drawings of snakes, lizards, men, and geometric figures. Drive nine miles west of Gila Bend on Interstate 8, then nine miles north on the marked access road. Open daily, year round; admission is charged.

Picture Rocks Retreat includes a short, well-maintained path that leads to a tall, exposed rock area, on which a variety of petroglyphs can be seen. The Redemptorist Fathers maintain the site and welcome visitors. From Interstate 10 at the north edge of Tucson, turn west on Ina Road. At the intersection with Wade Avenue, turn left and drive about a mile to the site entrance. Open daily during daylight hours; admission is free.

San Carlos Apache Reservation (San Carlos 35550; 602-475-2361) is the next-door neighbor of the White Mountain Apache reservation. Venturing east from Phoenix toward the Petrified Forest on U.S. 60 and AZ 77; or south toward New Mexico on U.S. 70, you'll travel across this Apache homeland. The tribe owns all the concessions surrounding the 13,000-acre San Carlos Lake, which is popular with boaters, skiers, and fisher folk. (Contact: Box 24, Peridot 35542; 602-475-2756.)

Sunset Crater National Monument (Rt. 3, Box 149, Flagstaff 86004) was the center of volcanic eruptions that took place between 1064 and 1065 A.D. From Flagstaff, drive 15 miles northeast on U.S. 89, then follow directional signs on the paved loop road. The visitor's center is open daily; admission is free. Camping is permitted.

Three Turkey Ruin Tribal Park is an Anasazi site that was occupied for only a little more than 50 years, apparently by people who came from Mesa Verde at about the time that area was being abandoned. From Chinle, at the edge of Canyon de Chelly National Monument, drive south five miles on Arizona 7 to directional sign, then five miles west on a primitive road to the Three Turkey Overlook. Open daily, except in bad weather; admission is free.

Tonto National Monument features cliff dwellings that were inhabited nearly 600 years ago. Visits to the Upper Ruin can be made only through guided tours, which must be arranged four days in advance. Open daily; admission is charged.

Tumacacori National Monument was declared a national monument in 1908. A mission church of San Jose de Tumacacori built around 1800, it is located a few miles north of Nogales on Interstate 19.

Tuzigoot National Monument offers visitors a self-guided tour of this prehistoric hilltop town, which once consisted of nearly 100 rooms. Tuzigoot is located between Clarkdale and Cottonwood on AZ 279 and U.S. Alt 89. Open daily; admission is charged.

Walnut Canyon National Monument (Rt. 1, Box 25, Flagstaff 86004; 602-526-3367) also features a self-guided tour along the rim of Walnut Canyon, then down to 25 cliff-dwelling rooms. From the trail, about 100 other dwellings can be seen. From Flagstaff drive 7 1/2 miles east on Interstate 40 to directional sign, then three miles southeast to visitor's center. Open daily; admission is charged.

Walpi is a Hopi Indian village, built on top of a high mesa. Some of the dwellings go back at least 300 years, and remains of prehistoric houses lie on the slopes below the present village. From Tuba City at the junction of U.S. 164 and Arizona 264, drive southeast at the directional sign. Camping is available nearby.

The **White Mountain Apache** are one of the few American Indian nations to operate their own ski resort, **Sunrise** (located between McNary and Eagar on Route 273), which explains why so many non-Indian motels, condominiums and private cabins exist on the northern edge of the reservation by Pinetop-Lakeside. Call 800-55-HOTEL or 602-735-7600 for ski area information.

Wupatki National Monument includes about 800 ruins, nearly 100 of them within a one-square-mile area. From Flagstaff, drive 32 miles north on U.S. 89 to the Wupatki-Sunset Crater Loop Rd. entrance, then 14 miles east to the visitor's center. Open year round; admission is free. Camping is available nearby.

CALENDAR OF EVENTS

JANUARY
- The **King's Day Inauguration** takes place at most pueblos during the first week of the month.
- The **Kiva and Buffalo Dances** are performed in Hopi villages during the last week of the month.

FEBRUARY
- **O Dam-Tash Indian Day** and an **Indian Rodeo** take place during the third week of the month in Casa Grande. Call the Casa Grande Chamber of Commerce, (602) 836-2125, for information.
- During the last week of February, the **Bean Dances** are performed in kivas at Hopi villages.

MARCH
- The **Indian Dance Festival** at St. John's Mission on the Gila River Reservation is scheduled for early in the month.
- During the second week, the **Mul-Chu-Tha Fair and Rodeo** takes place in Sacaton.
- The **Indian Market** is held in Phoenix during the third week of the month. Call (602) 253-1594 for information.
- In the last week of March, the **Pima Trade Fair and Dances** take place on the Salt River Reservation.
- The **Chinle Agency Navajo Song and Dance** is also held in the last week of the month as part of the **Pow Wow Festival** in Chinle. Call (602)674-5201 for information.
- During Easter week, the **Yaqui Dances and Pageant** are held in Pascua and Tucson, and the **Festival of St. Francis** takes place in the Yaqui Village in Tucson.

APRIL
- **Spring Corn Dances** are held at all pueblos during the first week of April.
- The **Indian Rodeo** takes place in the first week of the month in Sacaton.
- On the second weekend of the month, an **Indian Rodeo** is held in Tsaile.

APRIL (continued)

- During the third weekend, you'll find another **Indian Rodeo** in Tuba City.
- A powwow at the **San Xavier Reservation** in Tucson is open to travelers late in the month.
- The **Navajo Area Native American Festival** at Many Farms High School in Many Farms also takes place late in the month. For information, call (602) 781-6226.

MAY

- There's an **Indian Rodeo** somewhere in Arizona during every weekend in May. The first weekend, rodeos are staged at Ganado and Kayenta; the second weekend, in Fort Defiance and Kayenta; the third weekend, in Ganado; the fourth weekend, in Tuba City and Pinon.
- On Memorial Day, **Indian Dances** take place on the Havasupai Reservation and an **Indian Fair** is held in Flagstaff.
- The **KTNN Song & Dance Festival** is celebrated at the Navajo County Fairgrounds in Holbrook during May. Call (602) 871-2666 for information.

JUNE

- Weekend **Indian Rodeos** continue during June. The first weekend of the month, there is a rodeo in Oraibi; the second weekend, in Selba Dalkai; the third weekend, in Houck; the fourth weekend, in Tsaile.
- During the first week of June, the **Yaqui Pageant** takes place in Sacaton.
- At mid-month, **Apache Ceremonials** are held on the San Carlos Reservation in Peridot.
- On the 24th, **San Juan's Day** is celebrated at the Papago Reservation.
- The **Flagstaff Festival of Native American Arts**, at the Coconino Center for the Arts in the County Court House, begins in June and runs through August. Call (602) 779-6921 for information.
- The **Flagstaff Indian Days Pow Wow** is held in June. Call (602) 779-6131 for information.
- **Navajo Nation Treaty Day** is celebrated in June at Window Rock. Call (602) 871-6436 for information.

JULY

- More **Indian Rodeos** highlight the month of July. From the first through the fourth, a rodeo takes place at Window Rock, culminating in the **Celebration PRCA Rodeo** on the fourth. On the first weekend of the month, there are rodeos in Window Rock and Whiteriver; on the third weekend, in Lukachukai; on the fourth weekend, in Whiteriver.
- On the fourth of the month, **Feasts, Games & Races** are held at most pueblos.
- Late in the month, **Niman Kachina** is celebrated at Hopi villages and the **Saguaro Festival** takes place on the Papago Reservation.
- The **Western Navajo Fair** is a July event in Tuba City. Call (602) 283-5452.

AUGUST

- During the third week, the **Havasupai Peach Festival** is held in Supai.
- The third weekend of the month, there is an **Indian rodeo** in Sawmill.
- During the fourth week, the **Hualapai Powwow** in Peach Springs is open to the public and the **Apache Fair**, featuring the **Crown Dance**, is held in Whiteriver.
- Late in the month, the **Snake Dance** is performed at Hopi pueblos.
- Also in August, the **Central Navajo Fair** is held in Chinle. Call (602) 674-5673 for information.
- The **Handweavers Guild Exhibit and Sale**, is held in August at the Museum of Northern Arizona in Flagstaff.

SEPTEMBER

- From the third to the sixth, the **Apache Fair** is held in Whiteriver.
- Early in the month, the **Navajo Tribal Fair** takes place at Window Rock.
- The first weekend of the month, there is an **Indian Rodeo** at Whiteriver; the second weekend, at Window Rock; the third weekend, at Fort Defiance.
- Late in the month, an **Indian Fair** takes place at Tuba City.
- The **Southwestern Navajo Nation Fair** takes place in Dilcon. Call (602) 657-9244 for information.

SEPTEMBER (continued)

- The **Annual Navajo Nation Fair** is held in Window Rock. Call (602) 871-6702 for information.

OCTOBER

- On the fourth, the **Feast of St. Francis** is celebrated at the Papago Reservation.
- **Indian Rodeos** are held the second weekend of the month, in Tuba City; the third weekend, in Phoenix; and the fourth weekend, in San Carlos.
- **Ceremonial Dances** are performed late in the month at most pueblos.
- The **Western Navajo Fair** takes place in Tuba City. Call (602) 238-5452.
- The **Coyote Calling Contest** is held in Window Rock. Call (602) 871-6451.
- The **Arizona Indian Living Treasures Exhibition** is featured in Sedona during October. Call (602) 282-8766 or (602) 282-4061 for information.

NOVEMBER

- Early in November, the **All-Indian Tribal Fair and Rodeo** takes place on the Papago Reservation.
- During the second weekend of the month, there is an **Indian Rodeo** in Sells.
- The **Heard Museum Craft Show** is held during the second weekend at the museum in Phoenix, 22 E. Monte Vista Rd., (602) 252-8848.
- At mid-month, the **Apache Memorial of Veterans** occurs in Peridot.
- The **Casa Grande Ruins Art Fair** is held in November at the Casa Grande Ruins Monument.
- The **Native American Art Festival,** a **Native American Dance Festival & Dinner,** and a **Tribute Pow Wow** are held at the Gila River Arts & Crafts Center. Call (800) 472-6298 for information.

DECEMBER

- During the first week of December, the **Pueblo Grande Museum Arts & Crafts Show** runs at the Pueblo Grande Museum, 48th & Washington, Phoenix, (602) 275-3452.

- From the second to the fourth of the month, the **Feast of St. Francis** is celebrated at San Xavier.
- On the first weekend of the month, an **Indian Rodeo** takes place in Parker; on the second weekend, there is a rodeo in Chinle.
- During the week prior to Christmas, the **Indian Water Festival** is held at the Colorado River Reservation in Parker.
- On the 25th, there is dancing in churches at all pueblos during **Midnight Mass; Deer and Matachines Dances** in most Pueblos; and the **Christmas Tree for Tribes** at the Colorado River Reservation in Parker.
- The **Annual Christmas Arts and Crafts** festival takes place this month in Window Rock. Call (602) 871-6376 for details.
- The **Navajo Night Way and Mountaintop Way Ceremonies** are held in Window Rock during December.

LIBRARIES

Amerind Foundation Research Library in Ragoon has 20,000 volumes focusing on American Indian ethnology, archaeology, and art.

Arizona Historical Association Library, in Tucson, has 35,000 volumes related to Arizona and the Southwest.

Arizona State Museum Library at the University of Arizona in Tucson includes 32,000 volumes of published and unpublished materials, field notes, and diaries related to Southwest archaeology and ethnology.

Canyon De Chelly National Monument in Chinle, the **Tuzigoot National Monument** in Clarksdale, and the **Wupatki National Monument** in Flagstaff have libraries as part of their facilities.

Casa Grande Ruins National Monument Library in Coolidge has 1,500 volumes on Hohokam archaeology and culture.

College of Law Library at the University of Arizona in Tucson holds a special collection on law relating to the American Indian.

Colorado River Indian Tribes Public Library in Parker has 25,000 volumes about the Navajo, Hopi, Mohave and Chemehuevi.

Harold S. Colton Memorial Library at the Museum of Northern Arizona in Flagstaff contains 10,000 books on Hopi and Navajo Indians.

Heard Museum Library in Phoenix owns 40,000 volumes of North American art and culture, with emphasis on the Southwest.

Hubbell Trading Post National Historic Site Library in Ganado includes materials relevant to Navajo culture, arts and crafts, and trading information.

Mission San Xavier Del Bac Library in Tucson has 5,000 volumes pertaining to Aztec and Native American ethnography and anthropology.

National Indian Training and Research Center Library in Tempe has 1,000 volumes relating to Indian education.

Native American Research Library in Window Rock includes 2,000 volumes and 1,000 manuscripts, films, tapes, and microfilm on Navajo Indians.

Navajo Community College Library in Tsaile features the Moses Donner Indian Collection, an extensive group of publications on Indians.

Navajo National Monument Library in Tonalea contains 600 volumes on Navajo history and archaeology.

Phoenix Indian Medical Center Health Sciences Library in Phoenix has basic professional and medical collections with a special collection on Indian health concerns.

Pueblo Grande Museum Library in Phoenix focuses its collection primarily on Southwest archaeology.

Smoki People Library in Prescott includes 600 volumes on North and South American Indian dance and ceremonials.

Southwest Folklore Center at the University of Arizona in Tucson is a good resource for Southwest Indian folklore.

State of Arizona Department of Library and Archives in Phoenix has a whopping 500,000 volumes, including much material devoted to Southwest Indians.

Stradling Museum of the Horse Library in Patagonia has 1,000 volumes on Indian history.

Western Archaeological and Conservation Center Library in Tucson has 15,000 volumes on archaeology, anthropology, and the history of Southwest.

Yavapai-Prescott Tribal Library in Prescott has a special Indian collection on the major Southwest tribes.

CAMPGROUNDS

You can find campgrounds at: the **Colorado River Reservation**, 5 miles north of Parker; the **Fort Apache Reservation**, 165 miles east of Phoenix; the **Fort McDowell Reservation**, 20 miles northeast of Phoenix on State 87; **Four Corners**, Four Corners Monuments; the **Havasupai Reservation**, on the floor of Grand Canyon; the **Hopi Reservation**, northwest Arizona, within the Navajo Reservation; the **Hualapai Reservation**, on the southern rim of the Grand Canyon, near Kingman; **Little Colorado River**, State 64, Navajo Peak, George Overlook; **Monument Valley**, Monument Valley Station; the **Navajo Reservation**, northeast Arizona, extending into New Mexico and Utah; **Papago Reservation**, southern Arizona on Mexico border; **Salt River Reservation**, east of Scottsdale; and the **San Carlos Reservation**, 120 miles east of Phoenix; **Tsaile South Shore**, south of Lukachukai.

NATIVE AMERICAN CENTERS

The following centers serve Native American communities in Arizona:

Native Americans for Community Action, Inc.,
2717 N. Steves Blvd., Flagstaff, (602) 526-2968.

Phoenix Indian Center,
99 E. Virginia, Suite 160, Phoenix, (602) 258-1260.

Tucson American Indian Association,
131 E. Broadway, Tucson, (602) 884-7131.

Winslow Indian Center,
407 E. 3rd St., Winslow, (602) 289-3986.

CRAFT GUILDS AND COOPERATIVES

Colorado River Indian Tribes Senior Citizens Clock Factory in Poston manufactures wall clocks with tribal designs from Mohave, Navajo, Chemehuevi and Hopi.

Hopi Arts and Crafts-Silvercraft Cooperative Guild in Second Mesa is a Hopi crafts cooperative featuring jewelry, baskets and kachina dolls.

National Native American Cooperative in San Carlos can locate all traditional native arts and crafts and raw materials for craftwork.

Papago Tribal Arts & Crafts Cooperative Guild in Sells specializes in coiled yucca basketry and horsehair miniature blankets by Papago craftspeople.

Navajo Arts and Crafts Enterprises in Window Rock features all kinds of Navajo crafts.

INDIAN NEWSPAPERS AND NEWSLETTERS

Indian newspapers and newsletters include: *Au-Authm Action News*, Scottsdale; *Fort McDowell Newsletter*, Fountain Hills; the *Gila River News*, Sacaton; *Indian Arizona Today*, Phoenix; the *Journal of American Indian Education*, Arizona State University, Tempe; the *Phoenix Indian Center Newsletter*, Phoenix; *Pima Maricopa Echno*, Sacaton; *Sleeping Red Giant*, Community Services, Sacaton; *The Thunderer*, American Indian Bible Institute, Phoenix.

STATE AND REGIONAL AGENCIES

The following state and regional agencies are concerned with Indian affairs:

Arizona Commission on Indian Affairs, Phoenix, (602) 542-3123.
Inter-Tribal Council of Arizona, Phoenix, (602) 248-0071.
Arizona Department of Education, Indian Education Division, (602) 542-4391.

TOURISM OFFICES

For tourism information about the Supai area in Arizona, contact **Havasupai Tourist Enterprises** (Havasupai Tribal Council, P.O. Box 10, Supai 86435; 602-448-2961 or 448-2731).

For information about native attractions throughout the state, contact **Native American Tourism Center** (4130 North Goldwater Blvd, Scottsdale 85251; 602-945-0771).

The Hualapai have the only down-to-the-river access to the Grand Canyon at Peach Springs. Tribal guides are required. At Peach Springs, the traveler can book one- or two-day Colorado River trips. Travelers must understand that the Hualapai are strict in requiring tribal permits for traveling off U.S. 66. Trespassing violations are prosecuted. Contact the **Hualapai Tribal Council** (P.O. Box 168, Peach Springs 86834; 602-769-2216) for details and permits.

The **Navajo Nation Tourism Office** (P.O. Box 663, Window Rock 86515; 602-871-6659) provides tourism information for events on the reservation.

Selected Attractions:

NATIVE ARIZONA

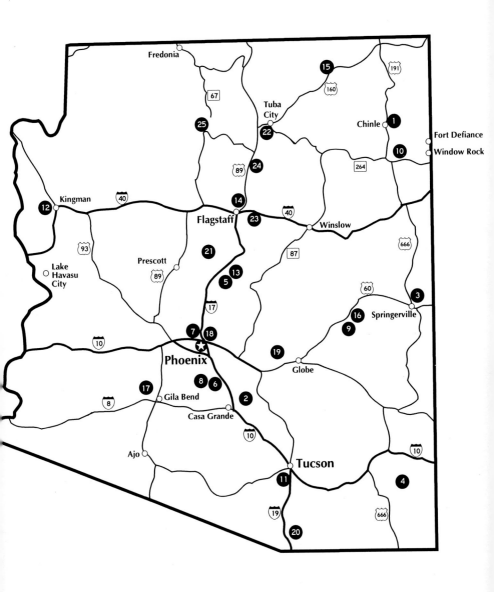

NEW MEXICO

INTRODUCTION

The state's very name poses a geographical, historical, and political dilemma. Is the "Mexico" in "New Mexico" relevant when it comes to understanding Native American heritage? For the most part, the answer is "no."

In geological terms, New Mexico is part of the watershed called the Colorado Plateau. This is not to imply that the many peoples who called the area home long before the Spanish called it "Nuevo Mexico" or archo-geologists described it as part of the Colorado Plateau didn't have their own names and boundaries.

Arizona has its special history, which places certain people in certain places at particular times. Colorado has its great backbone of 14,000-foot peaks and many mountain ranges. To define its natural boundaries, we call the area "the Rockies." Utah has its own history, and its own role to play in the history of southwestern Native American life.

None of these, though, is quite like what we now call New Mexico. Here we find the oldest-known evidence of the region's earliest inhabitants.

FOLSOM, CLOVIS, AND BEYOND

There is a small town in New Mexico called Folsom, which has no relation to the infamous prison. Folsom is at the end of a small road off Hwy. 64, which goes to Raton; the site itself is inaccessible by road and not open to the public. The Folsom site was "discovered" by George McJunkin, an African-American cowboy. There is a small museum in the town, open from June to October, which draws attention to McJunkin's life as well as the archaeologically ancient items including spearpoints that have been taken from the site.

Finding Clovis is an easier task. Near the Texas-New Mexico border, the Clovis site is located in a place called Blackwater Draw. Eastern New Mexico University manages the Blackwater Draw Museum, located between Clovis and Portales on U.S. 70. The site was discovered by a pair of amateur archaeologists, C.W. Anderson and George Roberts, who found unique stone points and the bones of mammoths. However, it wasn't until 1932 that a more knowledgeable expert in Carlsbad, Edgar

---

A Pueblo Indian dons a basket hat for a festival in Gallup, New Mexico.

Howard, drew the connection and understood the immense value of the parallel discoveries at Folsom and Clovis. Again, the site itself is closed, but the museum provides the traveler with essential background understanding of the lives of the Paleo-Indian hunters.

There were no maps about ten thousand years ago for those who left behind spearpoints—fluted, handmade killing instruments. Those travelers affixed hand-crafted points of different sizes to shafts or poles, and theorists believe these simple weapons were thrust toward giant creatures now aptly called mammoths. The key to the discovery of these points at Clovis is their "fluting."

These were carefully constructed weapons, fashioned by hunters who knew what was needed to do the job. They affixed the point to a shaft and wrapped it; then they had to locate a mammoth and thrust several of these spears into the hairy, gigantic mammal, whose tusks were easily twice their own height. If one wants a relatively comparative parallel, consider those early Native Americans and Europeans who sought to kill a whale.

How do we know this connection exists in Clovis? The points were found with mammoth bones. What was the value of "fluting?" A quantum increase in accuracy and penetration resulted from the points.

In what we now define as New Mexico, we find evidence of at least 11,000 years of citizenship. There are points found in Texas that pre-date the Clovis and the Folsom cultures; for example, those found in Lewiston date from possibly 40,000 years ago. And in the Old Crow Flats of Canada's Yukon Territory, caribou-bone implements were found that date around 27,000 years ago.

Was there a rivalry between those who are called "Folsom" and those who are designated "Clovis?" It's unlikely. And there is evidence of a people we call "Sandia" after the New Mexican mountain range where more spearpoints were found. These date the Sandia culture to at least 9500 B.C. They are most certainly remnants of the hunters who ranged the region, but there is a major leap between the Sandia hunting weapons and those of the Clovis and Folsom peoples.

The Clovis hunters, called so only because of the location where the points were found, existed about 1,000 to 2,000 years before the Folsom hunters, according to most estimates. That does not make the two groups historic enemies, nor does it necessarily make them ancestors. What sets the two apart is the crafting of their spearpoints, as well as other evidence found in areas where "lost" weapons have been located.

The Folsom points are so different from the Clovis points that nobody can do more than make educated guesses as to the origin and purpose of each design. The Clovis points are sharper, and their construction was obviously dedicated to fitting the points into a groove of the shaft, giving more power to the fashioned stone than it would have were it simply tied to the end of the "stick." Looking at the Folsom people's points, one wonders exactly why the fluting extends so far along the body of the point. Of course, we have no written instructions that come with each point, which makes the comparison even more intriguing.

Somewhere along the line in hunting history, the two peoples learned that one kind of point was more effective in bringing down one particular species of game or another. Some think hunters used their weapons in different ways: using the "slingshot" method of propelling a pointed shaft toward a quarry, for example, or using the sheer power of the arm to find vulnerable areas.

Petroglyph National Monument bears the markings of pre-Columbian tribes.

Whatever the differences between the Folsom, the Clovis, and the Sandia peoples, we know that they were hunters constantly on the prowl for game—for the great and small creatures that would sustain them by providing food, clothing, and practical resources. In academic language, these people are given the relative anonymity of "Lithic Indians," or Paleo Indians. What is important is that we now have significant evidence of their presence in what we now consider the American Southwest. In both the "Folsom-Plano Core Area" and the "Sandia-Clovis" area, there is impressive evidence that the people were habitual residents.

Climate, of course, affected the migratory patterns of ancient people and animals. Rains, snowstorms, droughts, melting icecaps, volcanic explosions—there were a multitude of reasons why groups of people would move from one place to another. When the grazing animals moved, so did the people. When the oceans dried up, the people moved inland or down the coast, where there the sea still existed. Hunter-gatherers did what they had to do to survive.

Their adaptability—a quality we now call intelligence—also helped them find ways to survive. No doubt, there were those who did not survive, caught in a whirlwind of sandy drought or the total desecration of natural harvests, flora, and fauna. But many found, within their own communities and their histories, the resources to forge ahead.

About 8000 years ago, life suddenly became more difficult. What were once habitats supporting great herds of animals and magnificent schools of fish, or great fields of edible plants, suddenly diminished to a bare minimum—if anything was left at all. There were those peoples who depended solely upon the relatively easy resources of their area, whether it grazed or grew. These Paleo-Indians had a hard time surviving.

Another group, today called the Archaic-Indians, was extremely survival-conscious. They went after anything and everything that would keep their people alive. Little animals, small plants, roots, shellfish—everything safe to eat was considered a blessing as well as a necessity. It took about 7,000 years for these southwestern survivors to learn that they could replicate what nature had given them. The knowledge that they could plant seeds and grow corn, squash, beans, and tobacco developed in Mexico and spread to the northern tribes.

There is a phenomenal place in New Mexico called "Bat Cave," situated within the "Cochise Core Area." Nobody knows exactly how or why—but there are some wise guesses—the Cochise learned to cultivate corn, but several small ears were found here that date to about 3500 B.C. This means that people were storing domestic harvests 5,000 years ago. There is evidence of similar and earlier harvests in Mesoamerica, in Mexico and countries south, and the Bat Cave site indicates a linkage between the "rural" cousins and their highly sophisticated brethren south of what we now call the Rio Grande.

Where does the contemporary traveler in New Mexico draw his or her boundary lines? This is the most sensitive question any traveler in Native America can ask. In New Mexico and the rest of the Southwest, one answer involves visiting and listening carefully to each culture, past and present, as it articulates or demonstrates the meaning of its own heritage. This is a road that will captivate the thoughtful traveler.

PUEBLO CULTURE

The contemporary names of the various peoples, of any tribe or nation, are typically bestowed by someone else. As mentioned numerous times in this guide, some names are openly hostile. "Sioux" was the French corruption of an Ojibwa word that meant "snake," as in snake-in-the-grass. "Pueblo" in Spanish simply means "village." Thus a multitude of different groups became "the Village People," because they lived in similar, elaborate communities.

Perhaps the most elaborate of all early southwestern communities is the one found near the eastern boundary of the Navajo Reservation in New Mexico and identified as Chaco Culture Historical Park. There is no easy way to reach Chaco. A quotation from a valuable park pamphlet warns, "ALL roads into the park are dirt for the last 20 to 26 miles . . . NO food, gas, lodging, or auto repair services are available at the park. Please plan ahead and arrive prepared!" Note that the nearest town is 60 miles away, a long way from Chaco.

It is always wise to call centers at Gallup (800-242-4282) or Farmington (800-448-1240) before venturing to Chaco. There are some 64 "first-come, first-served" campsites about a mile from the park's visitor's center, but bring your own firewood or charcoal. Gathering wood is illegal in Chaco. Water is only available at the visitor's center. Remember, too, that Chaco is 6,200 feet above sea level in what is called "high desert." That means you can expect very cold nights in winter and hot summer days. No pets are allowed. There are rules and regulations, a number of which carry steep fines if violated. All trails and ruins are off-limits after the sun sets. There is one eight-mile bicycle loop on the canyon floor, plus the roads and the "Wijiji" back country trail—otherwise, off-road riding is prohibited.

Why list the precautions before discussing the site's history? Partly because such warnings are essential knowledge for the traveler who plans to visit almost any portion of the Southwest's back country.

Chaco is quite possibly the most impressive and awe-inspiring Indian ancestral ruins north of Mexico. There are a dozen large ruins of pueblos or villages, plus one gigantic ruin. Some 2500 other sites are noted within the park. Trails lead to Pueblo Bonito, Chetro Ketl, Casa Rinconada, and Pueblo Del Arroyo. One does not simply stop by Chaco—it is an investment in time, energy, and patience, not to mention imagination.

The first step should be a stop at the visitor's center. There, one finds exhibits, books, and the park's helpful rangers who, in the summers, provide guided tours. Year-round, they provide not only information about the sites to be seen, but also a basic education concerning why Chaco is subject to all the laws and rules needed to preserve a World Heritage Site and a historical park.

A succession of doorways leads through the ruins of Pueblo Bonito in Chaco Canyon.

At the visitor center, there is an artist's rendition of Chaco's Pueblo Bonito, in what is thought to be its original shape and proportions. Few terms suffice to describe what once was a center of Anasazi culture, which existed for possibly eight centuries but flowered for two centuries (900-1100 A.D). The experts point to the early part of the 10th century as the time when the culture's acceleration really began.

Pueblo Bonito was a "planned" community that would eventually have somewhere between 600 and 800 rooms, all contained in what could be considered a half-circle or the letter "D." Possibly 1,000 people lived here—the 800 rooms of the multi-storied structure, though, contained (and still contain) the greatest collection of circular kivas found anywhere. In all, 40 of these round, pit-shaped constructions used in spiritual ceremonies are found here.

Another index of the Chaco/Anasazi evolution as builders and architects is the variety of building styles found here. While the plaster coatings have largely washed away over time, the durability of each type is amazing—both those using mortar and those using only rock shapes to maintain support for the stories erected above them. Even the experts

A full moon rises over Fajada Butte in Chaco National Historical Park.

disagree about why Chaco, which possibly supported 5,000 people at the height of the canyon's development, existed in the first place. Certainly, the variability of the climate and its temperatures, its relative aridity and its isolation from streams and rivers were minuses, rather than pluses. The nearest river is the San Juan, many thousands of footsteps away—however, the Chaco people did build a road to its banks.

Little original pottery has been found here, for the trade route that went through the canyon brought myriad other pottery styles to Chaco. The same cannot be said for jewelry, which explains part of Chaco's success as a trade center. There was a profusion of available turquoise in the area, transported to Chaco as raw ore, then transformed into brilliant works of art. In fact, more jewelry has been found in Chaco than at any other site in the Southwest.

Another outstanding ruin within Chaco is called Chetro Ketl, which apparently reached its developmental peak around 1050 A.D.—about the time the Normans were invading England—and which reflects some Mesoamerican influences. Chetro Ketl includes four unique kivas, two of which are far larger than those found in the canyon area and two that are "elevated" (above-ground), thus departing from the traditional pit style. Almost midway between Chetro Ketl and Pueblo Bonito is one of the largest kivas found in the Southwest. Casa Rinconada was apparently a "regional" ceremonial structure, for there is no sign of village life nearby significant enough to justify its solitary placement.

Traffic within the area moved along established roads, all leading to what is now the historical park. There are those who believe that Chaco's people acted as administrators of the entire region, while others believe that Chaco might have been the spiritual or ritual center for the Anasazi. There are many outlying villages and "satellite" communities directly linked to Chaco by roads and trails, which could have served as Chaco consulates. No one truly knows, but the existence of Chaco more than justifies profound respect for the place and its former citizens. Again, as with Canyon de Chelly or Mesa Verde, no one knows exactly why the place was fundamentally deserted by the 13th century. There are, again, indications that a half-century drought may have caused the culture to fracture under its own population needs and to move elsewhere in small groups. It's also possible that a combination of natural deprivation and "outside" non-Anasazi threats brought down a peaceful, agrarian, trading people's civilization and forced them to move.

An accessible "outpost" of the Chaco culture is found near Prewitt, New Mexico, at what are called the Casamero Ruins. The traveler reaches an unpaved county road that leads to a very identifiable power plant. The plant is the key to the site's discovery, for when the Bureau of Land Management was surveying land for the power generator, the BLM brought in "salvage archaeologists," just in case. These scientists uncovered one of the largest kivas in the Southwest, constructed in about 1050 A.D. Today the BLM manages the site and has a self-guided tour with a set of narrative signs to help the hiker learn more about this distant settlement more than 50 miles from Chaco Canyon.

There is no doubt that, either by bloodline or tradition, the people called the Pueblo today are linked to those of Chaco Canyon, Canyon de Chelley and Mesa Verde, among other major ruins that are built upon the Colorado Plateau.

While we refer generically to the Pueblo, it is critical to note that there are four different groups, each identified by the language it speaks: Tiwa, Tewa, Towa, and Keres. The first three are related to the Kiowa-Tanoan

The 800 rooms of the Pueblo Bonito ruins contain the greatest collection of circular kivas found anywhere.

93

language family. The Keresan language is, however, not related. In addition, these four were often subdivided and called by the place where they lived, as in the case of the Acoma or the Taos peoples. In the course of our exploration of New Mexico, there will be occasions when certain Pueblo groups will be identified by place and by language group. In the end, this should help the traveler find his or her way around what are fundamentally called the Pueblos.

Most Pueblo communities do not look like Acoma or Taos Pueblos. Some appear as very "ordinary" small southwestern towns. There are those called "reservations," but there are also "pueblos"—designated sites held through treaties with the U.S. government. Places like Acoma Pueblo, called "Sky City," is one place; the Acoma Pueblo Reservation is another; in the middle of the Pueblo Taos Reservation is the fabled Taos Pueblo. The Acoma and the Taos "villages" have been continuously inhabited by their people for more than a thousand years.

A visit to either of these pueblos is like stepping back through a window of time. Hopefully, the traveler can also visit Mesa Verde in Colorado, Chaco Canyon in New Mexico, or Canyon de Chelly in Arizona, for it is in this way that the connection to the Anasazi can be confirmed. Whether found atop a mesa, on flat land, or in the ancestral caves the sites all point directly to two of the primary earlier cultures, the Anasazi and the Mogollon peoples.

There are many connections, as well, with the Hopi and the Zuni, as well as the Rio Grande Indians. While building styles may have varied— the Pueblos are noted for their multi-storied structures with log beam roofs—the Hopi, the Zuni, and the different Pueblo groups all constructed ceremonial pits. While the Hopi and Zuni kivas might be scattered or distributed according to clans and families, the Pueblo generally tended to build theirs in the center of the village. Similarly, the Pueblo created masks and kachina dolls—the masks to represent gods and goddesses, and the dolls to be used as icons and as a way of instructing the children in the spiritual meanings of life.

As is to be expected, the influx of new peoples into the Colorado Plateau, its variable climate, and tribal populations that always seemed to be on the rise had their effects upon the individual groups. With the arrival of the Apache and the Navajo, life changed for the Pueblo people, to be sure, including the newfound need to defend their villages and outposts.

While these changes occurred over centuries, even epochs, there was nothing to rival the arrival of the Spanish. Within less than two decades, the conquistadors made their way from "New Spain" (later to be called Mexico) after its founding in the south to the Pueblo region.

In 1539, the Spanish were in Zuni territory. Coronado followed a year later in his vainglorious search for the fabled Seven Cities of Gold. As far as we know, these contacts had fairly little impact upon the Pueblo peoples, but this all changed within a half-century. In 1598, a colonist named Juan de Onate brought a large group of "civilians" to the area, and with them livestock, European agriculture, the Church, and a new name for the area: New Mexico.

By 1610, de Onate had established Santa Fe as the colonial capital. His "army" coerced the nearby Pueblo people into paying taxes, into "giving" bounties of cotton and cloth, and into forced labor. Meanwhile the Church sought to remove from the Indians all vestiges of traditional spiritual beliefs. The colonial ruler considered the native people crude pagans, and his punishments were often horribly executed. The normally pacific Pueblo peoples began to rebel.

Among the first to resist were the Keres, who called Acoma home. Their almost inaccessible, mesa-top pueblo allowed them defense for a short time, resulting in the deaths of several Spanish soldiers. De Onate avenged their killing with the massacre of hundreds at Acoma. Among those who survived, he punished all adult males by cutting off one of their feet; all boys and girls over 12 years old were sentenced to 20 years of slavery, and all younger children were handed over to missions. Acoma became the example used by the Spanish to quell any other protests against domination. The Indians, on the other hand, would use it to fuel rebellion.

In the Arizona chapter of this book, we examine in detail what is now called The Pueblo Rebellion of 1680. Briefly, though, a San Juan Tewa priest, Pope, protested the abolition of his religious practices. Pope contrived a simple but effective means of communicating a plan to attack the Spanish, drawing support from other villages throughout New Mexico, including what is now Arizona.

On August 11, 1680, the Native American peoples of the Southwest moved against all Spanish authorities, civil, military and religious. The Indians were victorious and saw the Spanish population leave their lands. For 12 years, the region was once again Indian Country. Then the Spanish returned, regained what they had lost, and ruled the Pueblos continuously for the next 130 years. Then the Mexican Revolution occurred, and Mexico became independent of Spanish rule. Now the Pueblos were controlled by the Mexican government—at least until 1848, when the U.S. won the Mexican War and New Mexico Territory was ceded in the treaty of Guadalupe Hildago. Now the Pueblo were controlled by a third government. During the Mexican War, though, the Tiwa of Taos had skirmished several times with U.S. troops in retaliation against the army's theft of livestock and produce as well as the kidnapping of Tiwa women.

CONTEMPORARY PUEBLO CULTURE

Today's four fundamental Pueblo groups—Tewa, Tiwa, Towa, and Keres—live within 19 "pueblos" or reservations. This can easily spell confusion for the traveler who is seeking to visit one particular group. However, directions have been wonderfully simplified by the creation of the Eight Northern Indian Pueblos Council, which not only coordinates and promotes the activities of three Tiwa and Five Tewa pueblos, but also publishes an excellent annual guide.

The *Visitor's Guide* not only describes the histories and attractions of the eight pueblos—Nambe, Picuris, Pojoaque, San Juan, San Idelfonso, Santa Clara, Tesuque, and Taos—but also provides the traveler with a calendar of events, dances, and feast days. The guide also includes a map of the northern sector, an honest appraisal of the way to buy jewelry, and recommended etiquette and protocol within the pueblos. There are even recipes and potential itineraries. In addition, the publication is chockful of advertisements for galleries and artists, and articles about craftspeople and pueblo lifestyles. There are seven other pueblos in New Mexico, however, and of course each has its own special history, charm, and attraction.

ACOMA PUEBLO

Near the top of every New Mexico traveler's list of destinations is "Sky City," or Acoma Pueblo. To appreciate the Acoma people's cultural longevity, one must consider that people began living atop the high mesa about 1,000 years ago and have definitely called the place home since 1075.

Today "Sky City" is graciously open to travelers, but it is the traveler's responsibility to honor and respect that millennia of history. Tours are considered "privileges granted by the Acoma Tribal Council and Tribal

Administration." Remember that the Acoma are a sovereign people, proud and distinct by nature and tradition. Tourists often believe that their presence is an honor and financial necessity, so they are insulted when informed that they cannot wander hither and yon, snapping photos and making jokes about the ways that others live. As in any sovereign nation, visitors are required to abide by the prevailing laws.

The Acoma diplomatically call this "Visitor's Etiquette." How gentle they are in their reminders that they have rules and regulations, legally enacted. These range from simply staying on the paved paths when leaving the pueblo to reading signs that say visitors are not allowed in specific areas. At Acoma cameras and video cameras are prohibited at all times. Some provisions may be made with the council, but there is never a photograph allowed during special feast days; in fact, visitors are sometimes not allowed on the mesa during these celebrations.

Pueblo Eagle Dancers perform for crowds at the Pueblo Cultural Center in Albuquerque.

TAOS PUEBLO

Which came first, Taos or the Taos Pueblo? At first it seems an absurd question. Surely any village that has been continually inhabited for some ten centuries takes the longevity prize. However, there is the somewhat haunting reality of the small western town also called Taos, which became a world-famous cultural community, attracting writers like D.H. Lawrence and artists such as Georgia O'Keeffe. There are apt parallels between the arts community and the arrival of Columbus: the Taos Pueblo existed as a living culture for centuries, only to be "discovered" by non-Indians who were intrigued by the pueblo's continuity and its "antiquated" lifestyle. There was no electricity, plumbing, or running water here; but the straight-line simplicity of the pueblo's multi-story architecture fit seamlessly into the natural landscape. It soon became fashionable to replicate this architecture in the town of Taos. Now they superficially resemble one another, and the unschooled visitor might well ask: Which came first, Taos or the Taos Pueblo?

Taos Pueblo offers ingredients that many people find important: It's accessible, non-threatening, unique, and vestiges of the "simple life" remain. However, the pueblo poses a few problems for tourists. Photography, for example. The people of the pueblo at first regarded the camera with suspicion; later, it became a community profit-generator. There is now a charge to bring in photographic equipment, and rules and regulations must be obeyed. Portions of the pueblo are off-limits to visitors.

Taos Pueblo is probably the most popular Native American destination for tourists, artists, and travelers. The Sangre de Cristo Mountains form an impressive backdrop, and there is fascinating historic evidence here of the Spanish, Mexican, and American attempts to subjugate the Taos people. Many ground-floor spaces have become shops. The people of the pueblo have not ignored the financial rewards that can be reaped by hosting the dominant culture; however, they have done so without selling their souls. For additional information, contact the office of Taos Pueblo Tourism (P.O. Box 1846, Taos, 87571; 505-758-8626).

Taos Pueblo is one of the most popular destinations for travelers in the Southwest.

JEMEZ PUEBLO

Jemez is considered one of the "Eight Northern Pueblos," but it is the only Towa-speaking group in the country. Jemez State Monument is special for not only that distinctive linguistic consideration. One must drive through the Jemez and Zia reservations on U.S. 44 if traveling between Santa Fe and Albuquerque. However, the Jemez Pueblo is on state Hwy. 4. The State Monument includes ruins of a village called Giusewa, which thrived in the 14th century. The traveler will find at Giusewa a trend evident in contemporary archaeology and anthropology. The "experts" know that the pueblo, which was home to ancestors of today's Jemez people, was very large. Three-story buildings have been excavated, and the nearby hot springs was undoubtedly used by the people and their visitors six centuries ago.

Jemez has not been fully explored, nor will it be. What appears to have been a very impressive village will remain simply that, an impression, for once the fundamental dimensions were revealed, excavation was stopped. This is in line with the trend in contemporary science—once the scientists or scholars recognize the nature of a site or ruin and its purpose, they leave the site intact. It is a commendable practice.

The Jemez Mountains form an impressive backdrop to the Jemez Pueblo.

The Jemez State Monument, which includes the Jemez Pueblo, is one of the most impressive natural settings in the Four Corners states. Placed in a narrow valley surrounded by mesas and mountains, the Jemez lived for many years in scattered settlements, according to clans or families.

In 1598 a Spanish priest was "assigned" to the Jemez, and a mission was officially established at about the time the Pilgrims landed at Plymouth. Part of the state monument includes the 17th-century Franciscan Church of San Jose de los Jemez.

The traveler should stop at the monument's visitor center, where Jemez Pueblo rangers provide their own interpretation of their people's history. The center also contains displays and exhibits, as well as performances of classical Jemez music. Explanatory markers assist travelers on a self-guided tour through the ruins.

SANTA CLARA PUEBLO

Santa Clara Pueblo is one of the most famous of the Pueblo's cultures, and is the site of the Puye cliff dwellings. Santa Clara is located near the town of Espanola on U.S. 84, and the ancient homes of the Puye are closely connected to the nearby Santa Clara Pueblo.

The cliff dwellings were built inside great sandstone caves formed by water thousands of years ago. For about three centuries, more than 1,000 people lived there and on the 7,000-foot mesa above the caves. Around 1500, as happened in many other cliff communities, the place was abandoned. There are three trails leading to the cave dwellings and the mesa. The largest ruin is a 740-room structure containing a ceremonial chamber and what is called the "Great Community House." There are both guided and unguided tours, with varying fees for each. There are also fees for sketching and for taking pictures.

The mesa-cliff dwellers moved to the lowlands of the Rio Grande Valley. These Pueblo continued their agricultural pursuits and were noted for their black and red, highly polished pots and clay objects, as they still are today. Travelers may tour the pottery studios and several shops where Santa Clara products are sold. Dance celebrations are held throughout the year as well.

It is almost impossible to calculate or record all of the Pueblo people's contributions to enlarging a traveler's understanding of Native America—even in New Mexico alone. Fortunately, there are many, many books, free pamphlets and magazines that are devoted to expanding one's knowledge and appreciation of what the area's early residents experienced and left behind for us to see.

New Mexico's 19 pueblos reflect many differences in cultural creations, such as arts and crafts, and in particular celebrations and feast days, but they all share the heritage of the Anasazi.

ZUNI CULTURE

As noted in the Arizona chapter, the Zuni are also a Pueblo people. Their largest reservation is in New Mexico, as is their tribal headquarters. There are those who will merely say the Zuni or *Ashiwi* are Pueblo—no different from others save for the fact that their language is not Tiwa, Tewa, Towa, Keres, Hopi or Navajo. Since a people's language has proven time and time again to define their specific cultures, the *Ashiwi* are a most distinct group. The word "Zuni" is the name of a river that runs through a portion of northwestern New Mexico; "Ashiwi" is that people's term for "the flesh," or "that which surrounds the bones."

One way to look at a culture is through its various artistic interpretations of spirits and icons, the peculiar use of certain traditional designs or materials, and the fierce protection of certain celebrations. In these regards, the Zuni are unique. Most historians link Coronado's search for the Seven Cities of Gold to the locations of the original Zuni pueblos.

The Zuni today are noted for their artistically unique masks, exquisite silver and turquoise jewelry, and their special pots. Anyone interested in the differences between Colorado Plateau artisans should certainly visit Arizona's two exceptional museums, The Heard Museum and the Museum of Northern Arizona, as well as New Mexico's fine museums in Sante Fe and Albuquerque.

Is there anything specific that sets the New Mexico Zuni apart from the Zuni that once inhabited Arizona? There were seven pueblos in the 16th century, but one century later only three had endured the battles over territory: Halona, Matsaki, and Kiakima. Eventually, only Halona survived.

None of the original communities exist, save for this Zuni Pueblo near Black Rock (NM Hwy. 53), which has its particular beauty and its history restored. Another memorable site is the sacred Zuni Salt Lake, fifty miles south of the reservation, found in the crater of an old volcano which has long provided the Zuni and other tribes with a treasured, tradable commodity: salt.

A Zuni woman displays the exquisite jewelry and pottery for which the Zuni are known.

Within the established Zuni Reservation in McKinley County, the traveler finds well-named (in Spanish) communities that reflect the colonial settlements allowed or endowed by the Spanish, Mexican, and American governments: Nutria, Ojo, and Pescado. Today, one may fish the Rio Pescado, a series of lakes including Nutria and Eustice, or hunt in the Zuni valleys and around Corn Mountain.

Public events held today still reflect the uniqueness of Zuni culture. In the final days of August or the first ones of September, there is an annual Zuni fair. The Shalako Festival that occurs in late November or early December features a blessing of Zuni homes by great bird kachina dancers. All travelers should be aware of the various prohibitions and conditions regarding any kind of recording—on film, paper, or tape—of special ceremonies.

Zuni buffalo dancers.

APACHE CULTURE

The Apache emigrated south around 1300 A.D. The forces that caused this change of homeland, which would soon bring the people now called "Navajo" south as well, are not easily traced through Apache language or oral histories. But at some point in time in the first millennium, we know that an entire group of people who spoke a similar language ventured north, south, and southwest.

The Zuni people were tormented and terrified by the Apache—so much so that the Zuni word *apachu*, or "enemy," gives us these people's contemporary name. There seems to be no question that the "invasion" of a people who spoke a very different language than the regional residents— one identified as originating in western Canada—wrought havoc among the Anasazi, Sinaguan, Mogollon, and Hohokam peoples. The most significant

factor to consider in this dispersal of a broad and numerous group of people who spoke the same language is the real impact they had upon the areas in which they settled.

Of course, for many centuries across the North American continent, cultures were forcing themselves upon others. The newcomers often dominated. They won both land and captives. They killed, looted, and forced others to be subservient or to move on. The first 19 centuries of our continental history are filled with such initiatives.

Perhaps as a result of these invasions, the Hohokam vanished as a traditionally identifiable group, perhaps blending with other, more dominant groups as dying civilizations have done around the globe. The Mogollon, the Anasazi, and the Sinaguan peoples also became synthesized into other cultures that either required or encouraged assimilation in order to survive—individually, as families, as language groups, and as spiritual entities.

This has been a fact of cultural history from the beginning of time. It might not embody Darwin's "survival of the fittest," but it definitely demonstrates that the more vigorous and aggressive cultures survive.

When the Apache entered the Colorado Plateau, they brought with them two essential elements that would sustain their own people for almost a thousand years and that would encourage other people to reflect upon alternative means of survival. It's unfortunate that we—Indian and non-Indian alike—often regard the Apache people only as heroes who fought to the last man, woman, and child. Their gift to Southwestern culture extends far beyond their diminishing power and strength.

The Apache never relinquished their sense that they were entitled to personal and familial survival. They were not afraid to confront anyone or any group that challenged their desire to circumscribe tribal territory. The Apache also possessed a tenacity that enabled them to absorb elements of different cultures that would enhance their own ability to survive.

Dispersal was the key element in Apache survival. They came out of Canada in bands, clans, or families. Like the Hopi and many other people, they separated themselves—for purposes of self-identification and self-protection—by creating dialects and territories.

This guide has already discussed some of the Apache's history in the Southwest in the Arizona chapter. In what is now New Mexico, there are several significant Apache language groupings. Here one finds the Chiricahua, the Membrano, and the Jicarilla. This constitutes one-fourth of the variety of Apache dialects, all of which construct their own communities and cultures. As is noted in *The Encyclopedia of Native American Tribes*: "In the case of the Apaches, it is important to try to keep the band names straight rather than lumping them all together because, in the Apache Wars, different bands fought different battles."

The so-called "Apache Wars" were unlike the conflicts in which French and British used opposing Indian nations to fight their colonial battles. For example, the classic "French and Indian War" was really a series of battles between Native American allies of the Kings of England and France. By contrast, the Apache Wars were a series of skirmishes and raids against whomever was in charge of the colonial government—Spanish, Mexican, American.

The Apache Wars represent one of the world's longest continuous periods of armed conflict. The fighting began in the mid-16th century; almost 250 years later, the Apache were still fighting incursions into what they considered their territory.

Non-Indian, post-Columbian history generally acknowledges about 150 years of Apache opposition to American settlement and domination. Consider the opposing logic that spawned the conflict: the U.S.A. defeated the Mexican government, and as a result the Guadalupe Hildago treaty was signed in 1848. The Apache regarded this as irrelevant. They had never signed treaties with the Mexicans or the U.S., so they felt that whatever land they claimed was theirs. The U.S. government disagreed, since the cartographic definition of territory in the treaty included Apache land. Conflict was perhaps inevitable.

In the 1860s, while Lincoln's blue-clad troops were fighting east of the Mississippi, one contingent had to wage battle in the Southwest, with a formidable Chiracahua Apache war chief named Cochise. Today the traveler may discover on the Arizona map a spot called Chiracahua, but the nation that belonged to Cochise's people only vaguely exists in what is called Apache Pass.

Cochise's father-in-law, a Mimbreno Apache named Mangas Colorado, joined the fight. There are many, many accounts of the battles and skirmishes between the Apache and the U.S. government. Mangas Colorado was killed while in captivity in 1862; Cochise would survive until 1874.

Afterward another Mimbreno Apache named Victorio, together with the Chiricahua leader Geronimo, carried on the fight, beginning in Arizona's San Carlos Reservation. Historians have identified the conflicts, describing "Victorio's Rebellion" as having lasted from 1877 to 1880 and "Geronimo's Rebellion" as a stormy period between 1881 and 1886. These final Native American wars against the U.S. government represent, among other things, a valiant, against-all-odds defense of one's culture against overwhelming odds.

In many ways, the Apache still maintain their insistence upon their own lifestyles and open space. There are two Apache reservations in New Mexico, known for beautiful landscape, rushing streams, and hunting and fishing. The "Inn of the Mountain Gods" at Mescalero features a 200-room resort hotel overlooking a lake, an 18-hole golf course, stables, a skeet range, and a restaurant. At Jicarilla, a large hotel, cultural arts center, and performing arts stage are some popular attractions.

The traveler can take the few roads across the Jicarilla and Mescalero Apache reservations. Permits are required for hunting, fishing, and off-road adventures.

Mimbres (Mogollon) artifacts.

NAVAJO CULTURE

There is no group with a greater political, geographic, or economic presence among the Native Americans of the Colorado Plateau than the Navajo nation. That nation is the continent's most populous Indian group, containing almost a quarter-million people. It possesses the largest land commitment in the U.S., at about 18 million acres. The Navajo nation extends into Arizona, New Mexico, Colorado, and Utah.

Interestingly enough, while Window Rock—the Navajo equivalent to Washington, D.C.—is in Arizona's pivotal corner with New Mexico, there are several Navajo "colonies" in the Land of Enchantment. Though connected, they are separate reservations, areas, or communities. There is no question, though, that they are *Dineh*, or "the people," and that where they live is *Dinetah*, or "home of the people."

There are separate reservations for two bands of the Navajo in New Mexico: the Ramah and the Alamo Reservations. These, however, are

A Navajo wedding basket features striking abstract designs.

considered "chapters" of the greater Navajo Nation, and if one considers the distances from the farthest western chapter of the Navajo Reservation to Window Rock, the two reservations in Ramah and Alamo are not so removed from the central national council.

The Ramah tribal council, however, serves the Navajo of New Mexico. The Ramah Reservation is directly adjacent to the Zuni Reservation, (with NM Hwy 53, west, crossing out of Grants, off I-40), while the Alamo Reservation is less accessible, located in the Cibola National Forest (going north on NM Hwy 169, off U.S. 60, from Magdalena).

Possibly the most significant attraction adjacent to the Ramah Reservation is El Morro National Monument, which is fundamentally a Zuni and Pueblo landmark. Here the traveler will find a 200-foot sandstone pinnacle containing a multitude of Zuni petroglyphs that were carved long before the arrival of the conquistadors. To a significant degree, these etchings mirror contemporary Zuni designs and symbols found on jewelry, pottery, weaving and basketry as well as kachina masks. Seeing them adds a different dimension to one's appreciation of contemporary applications. Visitors will also see graffiti left behind by the Spanish explorers and by the soldiers of U.S. Army's camel cavalry.

El Morro, or "Inscription Rock," also includes two pueblo ruins on top of the mesa behind the high rock formation. There is a natural catch basin or pool at its base, used for centuries by the people of the two pueblos. The Spanish called it "El Estanque de Penol," and were frequent visitors, as were all subsequent travelers, random hunters, and wagon trains headed for California. Since this is a national monument, there are strict restrictions regarding the ruins and the petroglyphs, and only one of the ruins has been partly restored for visitors. There is a charge for using the various footpaths or trails, but no fee for entering the monument, which is open year-round. At the monument's visitor center, the traveler may pay to hike or camp.

A Navajo girl wears a dazzling display of silver and turquoise jewelry.

CONCLUSION

New Mexico's Native American history is rich with evidence of the cultures whose descendants one meets today in travels throughout the Southwest or the Four Corners region. One may find out the extent of the contemporary and ancient resources at parks and monuments, at tribal cultural centers, and at the universities and museums that are abundant throughout the state.

The various Native American centers (see listings at the end of this chapter) are important sources of information about events and new developments in the various Native American communities, pueblos, and reservations. Albuquerque, for example, hosts the Indian National Rodeo Finals in late November, replete with feasts, a powwow, and an arts and crafts sale. Gallup holds an Inter-tribal Ceremonial that begins on the second Thursday of August and has been going on for seven decades or more. This event includes a powwow, its own rodeo, a marketplace, barbecue, exhibits,

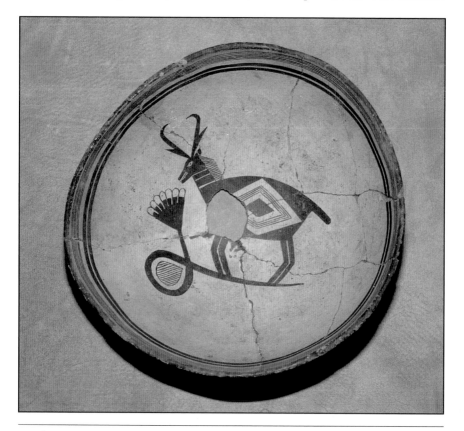

Mimbres pottery bowl.

beauty contests, performing arts presentations, and a half-marathon.

From Memorial Day through Labor Day, Native American dances are held every night in the Red Rock State Park, co-sponsored by the Ceremonial Association, the local chamber of commerce, and the state park. In September, Gallup also offers the successive Bi-County, Zuni, and Navajo Nation Fairs.

Farmington is the ideal location for finding out about the many Native American activities in northern New Mexico. The thriving town of nearly 40,000 residents is situated at the hub of the Navajo Reservation, just south of Colorado's Ute Mountain and Southern Ute Reservations. Mesa Verde and lesser-known ruins are located near Farmington; a half-dozen miles away is the Navajo Agricultural Products Industry, a 53,000-acre non-reservation operation. Farmington is not far from the Jicarilla Apache Reservation, the Four Corners National Monument, Chaco Canyon, Canyon de Chelley, and even Monument Valley.

These houses form part of the Acoma Pueblo, known as "Sky City."

MUSEUMS, ARCHIVES, AND CULTURAL CENTERS

Acoma Museum (P.O. Box 309, Acomita 87034) is a museum of Indian history and culture with photo archives and documents relating to the history of Acoma Pueblo. Open year-round. Admission is charged.

Coronado State Museum (P.O. Box 95, Bernalilo 87004) is the site of a partially reconstructed Pueblo Indian village ruin occupied circa 1300 to 1600. It includes a completely restored underground ceremonial kiva.

Deming Luna Mimbres Museum (301 S. Silver, Deming 88030) features exhibits of Mimbreno Indian artifacts and pottery.

Gallup Museum of Indian Arts and Crafts (103 W. 66th Ave., Gallup 87301) displays artifacts, arts, and crafts of the Navajo, Hopi and Zuni Indians.

Hardwood Foundation of the University of New Mexico (Ledoux St., Taos 87571) contains artifacts pertaining to Zuni, Taos, Apache, Cheyenne, and Ute tribes.

Indian Pueblo Cultural Center (2401 12th St. NW, Albuquerque 87102) preserves the traditions of the pueblo culture through a variety of

Works like this Parrot Pot from the Acoma Pueblo are on display at the Acoma Museum.

displays, collections, and demonstrations. It maintains archives pertaining to Southwest Indians and includes a museum, restaurant, and gift shop.

Institute of American Indian Arts Museum (Cathedral Place, Santa Fe 87501) contains approximately 6,000 items, including paintings, graphics, sculptures, ceramics, jewelry, textiles, and ethnological material of Native American students' work.

Jicarilla Arts and Crafts Museum (P.O. Box 147, Dulce 87528) displays basketry and other crafts. Open Monday through Saturday. Admission is free.

Kit Carson Historic Museums (P.O. Drawer B, Old Kit Carson Rd., Taos 87571) feature three museums, the home and art studios of Ernest Blumenschein, Kit Carson's adobe home, and the hacienda of Don Antonio Severino Martinez.

Maxwell Museum of Anthropology on the University of New Mexico Campus (University and Ash NE, Albuquerque 87131) features exhibits of Navajo weaving, Mimbres and Pueblo pottery, Hopi kachinas, and North American Indian basketry.

This Navajo sandpainting is one of the more ephemeral art forms preserved in New Mexico museums.

Millicent Rogers Museum (P.O. Box A, Taos 87571) offers a superb collection of prehistoric and historic Southwest and Plains Native American art and examples of material culture.

Museum of Indian Arts (708 Camino Lejo, Santa Fe 87504) consists of over 15,000 ethnographic objects and more than 26,000 archaeological objects, with emphasis on artifacts from the prehistoric, ethnographic, and present-day Indian Southwest.

Museum of New Mexico Fine Arts Museum (127 E. Palace Ave., Santa Fe 87501) features pottery, jewelry, and traditional attire of the Southwest, plus contemporary mixed-media art.

Paleo-Indian Institute of Eastern New Mexico University (P.O. Box 2154, Portales 88130) has exhibits and artifacts illustrating the life of the paleo-archaic and modern Indian, especially of Clovis Man, from the world-renowned Blackwater Draw archaeological site nearby.

Picuris Pueblo Museum (P.O. Box 228, Penasco 87553) displays pottery, beadwork, weaving, and other local crafts.

Red Rock Museum (P.O. Box 328, Church Rock 87311) in Red Rock State Park exhibits crafts and artifacts of prehistoric Anasazi and Navajo, Hopi, Zuni, Rio Grande Pueblos, Apache, and Plains Indians.

San Ildefonso Pueblo Museum (Rt. 5, Box 315-A, Santa Fe 87501) has a permanent collection of contemporary San Ildefonso Pueblo art, as well as prehistoric and historic Tewa art and artifacts.

San Juan County Archaeological Research Center and Library at Salmon Ruin (No. 975, U.S. Highway 64, Farmington) features artifacts from the Anasazi ruin, and an extensive on-loan collection of Navajo legends, myths, chants, and religious ceremonies.

The Wheelwright Museum of the American Indian (704 Camino Lejo, Santa Fe 87505) features collections of Navajo textiles and silver, Pueblo pottery, and reproductions of Navajo sandpaintings.

Zuni Archaeology Program (P.O. Box 339, Zuni 87327) maintains archaeological site records with comprehensive map files and air photos of the reservation and surrounding areas. Unpublished manuscripts on Zuni history and archaeology are also collected here.

PUEBLOS

Acoma Pueblo offers events open to the public from February to December. An official guide and calendar may be obtained from the Acoma tourist visitor's center (P.O. Box 309, Acoma 87034; 800-747-0181). There

This storyteller figurine was crafted by an artist from the Isleta Pueblo.

is a museum, with fees charged for tours of Sky City or San Esteban del Rey, a mission, a food concession, and a crafts shop. Tours vary according to the season, except July 10 through 13 and the first or second weekend in October, when special events take place. As with many Native American communities in the Southwest, there is a fee charged for bringing a camera on those days when it is permissible.

Santa Clara Pueblo (P.O. Box 580, Espanola 87532; 505- 753-7326) is quite organized, with its own tourism department and recreational area in the canyon; four lakes and a stream are open for trout fishing. There are fees for fishing, picnicking, sightseeing and camping.

Taos Pueblo (P.O. Box 1846, Taos 87571; 505-758-8626) is New Mexico's most popular Native American tourist destination. The pueblo includes shops, photo opportunities, dances and ceremonies, and unique pueblo architecture. There is a charge for photography, and visitors must obey pueblo rules and regulations.

Cave houses within the 29,000 acres of ruins at the Bandelier National Monument.

MONUMENTS, HISTORIC SITES, AND PARKS

Aztec Ruins National Monument (P.O. Box 640, Aztec 87410) along U.S. 550, includes a prehistoric Pueblo Indian ruin and features Anasazi artifacts from excavation sites within the San Juan Basin.

Bandelier National Monument in Los Alamos has approximately 29,000 acres of Anasazi Pueblo ruins, dating from 1200 A.D.

Chaco Culture National Historical Park (Star Route 4, Box 6500, Bloomfield 87413; 505-786-5384) is a world heritage site and features 13 major prehistoric Anasazi sites, and over 400 smaller villages sites. It is suggested that you write or call the park superintendent's office before a visit.

El Morro National Monument (Ramah 87321) is an archaeological site at Inscription Rock, featuring prehistoric Pueblo ruins.

Heritage Park, two miles west of Bloomfield on NM 64, is composed of eight habitation units nearly 2,000 years old.

Pecos National Historical Park features prehistoric Pueblo ruins and the remains of two Spanish churches.

Jemez State Monument (505-829-3530) features 12th-century Pueblo ruins and a 16th-century Spanish mission ruin. It is open year-round, and there is no charge from Thursday through Monday except on some holidays. There are camping facilities nearby, but permits must be obtained from the Forest Service.

Pecos National Historical Park (P.O. Drawer 418, Pecos 87552) contains prehistoric Pueblo ruins and the ruins of two Spanish churches. The visitor's center features 15,000 artifacts excavated between 1915 and 1929 from Pecos Pueblo. Elsewhere in the park are remnants of a six-mile section of the Santa Fe Trail.

Salinas Pueblo Missions National Monument (Rt. 1, Box 496, Mountainair 87036) is composed of three sites containing prehistoric pithouses dating to 800 A.D.; prehistoric Indian ruins dating from 1100 to 1600 A.D.; and Spanish Mission ruins circa 1627-1672.

CALENDAR OF EVENTS

JANUARY

- On New Year's Day, the **Corn, Turtle, and Other Dances** are performed at most pueblos, and the **Transfer of Canes of Authority to New Officers** ceremony is also held.
- On the sixth, the **King's Day Celebration** is held at most pueblos, and the **Deer or Buffalo Dance** is performed at Taos Pueblo.
- On the 22nd, **Evening Firelight Dances** are held at most pueblos.
- The **San Ildefonso Pueblo Feast Day,** featuring **Comanche and Animal Dances,** takes place on the 23rd at San Ildefonso Pueblo, 20 miles north of Santa Fe.
- On the 27th, the **Basket Dance** is performed in San Juan.
- Late in the month, the **Governor's Fiesta** is celebrated at Acoma Pueblo.

FEBRUARY

- On the second, **Buffalo Dances** and the **Candlemas Celebration** are held at Cochiti, Santo Domingo, and San Felipe pueblos.
- During the first week of the month, **Los Comanches** is celebrated at Taos Pueblo, featuring dances commemorating historical ties with the Comanche.
- At mid-month, special dances are performed at **San Juan Pueblo.**

- Late in the month, the **Clan and Deer Dances** take place at San Juan Pueblo, and the **Evergreen Dances** are performed at Isleta Pueblo.

MARCH

- The 19th is **St. Joseph's Feast Day** at Old Laguna Pueblo.
- The **Celebration of Opening of Irrigation Ditches** occurs during Easter week at most pueblos.
- On Easter Day, there are **Easter Ceremonies** and foot races at most pueblos.
- Around Easter, the **Eight Northern Indian Pueblos Spring Arts and Crafts Show** takes place at the De Vargas Mall in Santa Fe.
- At Eastertime, **Keresan Dances** are performed at Cochiti Pueblo.

APRIL

- **Spring Corn Dances** are performed from the first to the fourth at most pueblos.

Zuni festivals are colorful, exhilarating events.

APRIL (continued)

- Around mid-month, **American Indian Week** is celebrated at the Indian Pueblo Cultural Center in Albuquerque.
- The **Gathering of Nations Powwow** is held at the University of New Mexico Arena in Albuquerque during the middle of the month.
- Late in the month, **Intertribal Dances** are held at the University of New Mexico in Albuquerque.

MAY

- The first of the month is the **San Felipe Feast Day**, featuring the **Corn Dance** with over 500 dancers at San Felipe Pueblo and a celebration at Taos Pueblo.
- During the first week, the **Spring Arts and Crafts Expo** is held at the State Fairgrounds in Albuquerque.
- Early in the month, **Corn Dance and Ceremonial Dances** are performed at Taos Pueblo; the **Corn Dance** is held at Cochiti Pueblo;

Indian rodeos are staged throughout the Southwest.

Santa Cruz Feast Day takes place at Taos and Cochiti Pueblos; and the Santa Maria Feast is held at McCarty's, Acoma Pueblo.

- There is a Mother's Day Celebration at the Indian Pueblo Cultural Center in Albuquerque at mid-month.
- The 13th is the Annual Feast Day of St. Anthony in Sandia.
- At mid-month, the San Ysidro Fiesta is celebrated at Taos Pueblo and a Mescal Roast is held at Living Desert State Park in Carlsbad.
- The third weekend of the month, an Indian Rodeo takes place at San Fidel.
- The Annual Feast for St. John the Baptist is celebrated in San Juan on the 23rd and 24th.
- The 29th is San Pedro's Day at Acoma, San Felipe, Santa Ana, and Santo Domingo pueblos.
- Late in the month, Spring Dances are held at Tesuque Pueblo.

JUNE

- An Indian Rodeo takes place at Tsa-Ya-Toh on the first weekend of the month.
- On the eighth, the Buffalo Dance is performed at Santa Clara Pueblo.
- On the 13th, there is a Feast and Corn Dance at Sandia Pueblo, and there are San Antonio Day celebrations at Juan, Cochiti, and San Ildefonso pueblos.
- Anasazi, the Ancient Ones, a musical drama, begins its run at the Lions Wilderness Park in Farmington at mid-month. The show runs through September.
- On Father's Day, a Multicultural Festival is held at the Indian Pueblo Cultural Center in Albuquerque.
- On the 24th, there is a Rooster Pull at Jemez Pueblo and there are San Juan's Day celebrations at San Juan, Taos, Isleta, Cochiti, Laguna, and Acoma pueblos.
- Late in the month, the New Mexico Arts and Crafts Fair takes place at the New Mexico State Fairgrounds in Albuquerque.
- Another Rooster Pull takes place on the 29th at Old Acoma.
- Also on the 29th, San Pedro's Day is celebrated at Santa Ana, San Juan, and Taos pueblos.

JULY

- From the third to the sixth, the Mountain Spirits Ceremony is held on the Mescalero Apache Reservation.

JULY (continued)

- In the first half of the month, the **Los Voladores-Aztec Dancers** appear at the Indian Pueblo Cultural Center in Albuquerque.
- The **Waterfall Ceremony** takes place on the fourth at Nambe Pueblo; other feasts, games, and races can be found at most pueblos.
- Around mid-month, the **Taos Pueblo Powwow** is held at Taos Pueblo.
- On the 14th, **San Bonifacio Feast Day** and the **Green Corn Dance** are celebrated at Cochiti Pueblo.
- **Indian Rodeos** are held the second weekend of the month in Thoreau; the third weekend in Crownpoint; and the fourth weekend in Rock Springs.
- At mid-month, the **Annual Eight Northern Pueblos Artists & Craftsman Show** takes place in San Juan.
- The **Southwest Culture Festival** is held around the middle of the month at New Mexico Highlands University.

- During the second half of the month, the **Pope Foot Race** takes place in San Juan; there is an **Arts and Crafts Fair** at the Acoma Tourist visitor's center; and the **Eastern Navajo Fair** is held in Crownpoint.
- The **Corn Dance** is performed from the 25th to the 27th at Taos Pueblo.
- On the 25th, there are **Santiago's Day Dances** at Santa Ana and Laguna pueblos; the **Corn Dance** is held at Cochiti Pueblo; and **Rooster Pulls** are scheduled at Acoma and Santo Domingo pueblos.
- On the 26th, the **Festival of St. Anne** is celebrated at Laguna Pueblo; and **Santa Ana Feast Day**, with the **Corn Dance**, takes place at Santa Ana, Taos, and Acoma pueblos.
- Late in the month there is a **Puye Ceremonial** at Santa Clara Pueblo and a **Cross-Country Relay Race** at Laguna Pueblo.

AUGUST

- There are **Indian Rodeos** on the first weekend of the month in Crownpoint; on the second weekend in Gallup; on the third weekend in Nageezi; and on the fourth weekend in San Fidel and Little Water.
- **Our Day of the Angels Feast Day** is celebrated on the second at Jemez Pueblo.
- On the fourth, the **Old Pecos Bull Dance** is held at Jemez Pueblo; and **Santo Domingo Feast Day**, with the **Ripe Corn Dance** featuring over 500 dancers, is celebrated at Santo Domingo Pueblo.
- From the 5th to the 10th, there are **Symbolic Relay Runs** at all pueblos.
- On the 10th, **San Lorenzo Feast Day** and the **Corn Dance** are celebrated at Picuris and Acoma pueblos. The **San Lorenzo Day Festival** is also held on the 10th at Laguna Pueblo.
- On the 12th, **Santa Clara Feast Day** is celebrated at Santa Clara Pueblo.
- On the second weekend of the month, the **Gallup Ceremonial** is held at Red Rock State Park near Gallup.
- At mid-month, there is an **Intertribal Indian Ceremonial** in Gallup and at the state park 7 miles east of Gallup.
- The **Feast of St. Anthony** and various dances are held at Mesita Village and Laguna Pueblo on the 15th.

AUGUST (continued)

- At Zia Pueblo, **Assumption Day** and **Corn Dances** are celebrated on the 15th.
- During the third weekend of the month, there is an **Annual Indian Market** on the plaza in Santa Fe, with over 800 Indian artisans in juried competition.
- Late in the month, there is a **Spanish Fiesta** at Isleta Pueblo.

SEPTEMBER

- **St. Stephen's Day** and the **Corn Dance** are celebrated on the second at Acoma Pueblo.
- On the fourth, **St. Augustine's Day** festivities and various dances take place at Isleta Pueblo.
- Also on the eighth, **The Nativity of the Blessed Virgin Mary's Feast Day** is celebrated at Laguna Pueblo and the Village of Encinal.
- For most of the month, the **New Mexico State Fair and Rodeo** takes place at the New Mexico State Fairgrounds in Albuquerque.
- From the 14th to the 16th, the **Ghost Dance** and a **Fiesta** are held on the Jicarilla Apache Reservation.
- The **Jicarilla Apache Fair**, including rodeos, powwows, foot races, and dances, takes place around mid-month at Stone Lake and Dulce, both on the Jicarilla Apache Reservation.
- The Laguna Pueblo hosts a **Fiesta** and **Harvest Dances** on the 19th, and a **Fiesta** and **Social Dances** on the 25th.
- Late in the month, the **New Mexico Country Western Dance Fiesta** takes place in Albuquerque.
- From the 28th to the 30th, the **Sundown Dance** is performed at Taos Pueblo.
- **San Geronimo's Feast Day** is celebrated on the 30th at Taos Pueblo.
- Late in the month, a **Fiesta** and **Harvest Dance** are held at San Juan Pueblo; the **Evergreen Dance** is performed at Isleta Pueblo.

OCTOBER

- On the fourth, the **Elk Dance**, a **Fiesta**, and **San Franciso's Feast Day** are celebrated at Nambe Pueblo.
- Early in the month, the **American West Celebration** is held at Washington's Ranch in Carlsbad.

- The 10th is a **Feast Day** at the Quarai Monument, Salinas Pueblos Missions, and in Mountainair.
- A **Harvest Dances Celebration** takes place around mid-month at Laguna Pueblo.
- Late in the month, there are **Ceremonial Dances** at most pueblos; and **All Hallows Day** is celebrated on the 31st at most pueblos.

NOVEMBER
- The 12th is **San Diego Feast Day** at Jemez and Tesuque Pueblos.
- At mid-month, the **Indian National Finals Rodeo** takes place at the Tingley Coliseum, located on the state fairgrounds in Albuquerque.
- The third weekend of the month, an **Indian Rodeo** is held in Albuquerque.

DECEMBER
- Early in the month, the **Shalako Ceremony** is celebrated at Zuni Pueblo.
- On the first weekend, the **Institute of American Indian Art Annual Student Sales Show** begins at the IAIA Museum in Santa Fe, running through January 31st.

DECEMBER (continued)

- From the 10th to the 12th, the Tortugas Indians celebrate the **Feast Day of our Lady of Guadelupe** in the village of Tortugas, outside Las Cruces.
- On the 12th, the **Matachines Dance** take place at Jemez Pueblo.
- Beginning the 17th, the ruins at Aztec Ruins National Monument are illuminated with *farolitos*—sand-filled paper bags with lighted candles—every night until Christmas Day.
- The **Procession of the Virgin** takes place on the 24th at Taos Pueblo.
- On the 25th, there is dancing in most churches at **Midnight Mass**; and the **Deer and Matachines Dances** are performed at most pueblos.
- The **Turtle Dance** takes place on the 26th at San Juan Pueblo.
- **Holy Innocence Day** is celebrated on the 28th at Santa Clara.
- On the 31st, the **Deer Dance** is performed at Sandia Pueblo.

LIBRARIES

Acoma Museum Library and Archives, at the Pueblo of Acoma in Acomita, has a collection including photographs and documents relating to the history of Acoma Pueblo.

American Indian Law Center Library, at the University of New Mexico School of Law in Albuquerque, maintains a special collection on American Indian law.

Anthropology Film Center Foundation Library in Santa Fe houses a collection of films produced by graduates of the Film Center training program. Many are films on Native American subjects.

Aztec Ruins National Monument Library, in Aztec, has 300 volumes on the ethnography and archaeology of Southwestern Indians and prehistoric Pueblo Indians.

Bandelier National Monument Library, in Los Alamos, includes 2,000 volumes on the archaeology of the Pueblo Indians.

Chaco Culture National Historical Park Library, in Bloomfield has resources covering the prehistory of the Chaco area, as well as journals, photographs, and records of historic periods.

El Morro National Monument Library, in Ramah, has 400 volumes on historic pueblos.

Gallup Indian Medical Center Library, in Gallup, has a collection of titles about the Navajo.

Gallup Public Library, in Gallup, has a collection of rare, out-of-print, and contemporary titles on the Navajo, Hopi, and Zuni.

Gila Cliff Dwellings National Monument in Silver City includes a visitor's center library with a collection of books on the prehistoric Mogollon Indians, archaeology, and natural history.

Institute of American Indian Arts Library—Native American Videotapes Archives, in Santa Fe, includes 12,000 volumes on North American Indian art, history, and culture; and 30,000 Smithsonian photographs of Native American cultures.

Kit Carson Memorial Foundation Library in Taos houses 5,500 volumes on the prehistoric Indian culture of Taos and the Southwest.

Maxwell Museum of Anthropology Clark Field Archives, at the University of New Mexico in Albuquerque, has 2,500 volumes on archaeology, anthropology and ethnology.

Museum of New Mexico Library, at the Museum of Indian Arts and Laboratory of Anthropology in Santa Fe, has 16,000 volumes, including journal holdings, that concentrate on Southwestern anthropology.

New Mexico State Library in Santa Fe includes 11,000 books on Southwest history.

San Juan County Archaeological Research Center and Library, at Salmon Ruin in Farmington, has 800 books, 1,100 pamphlets, 1,100 technical reports, and 35 oral tapes about Navajo history and culture.

The **Wheelwright Museum of the American Indian**, at the Mary Cabot Wheelwright Research Library in Santa Fe, has 10,000 volumes on the art, history, and religion of the Navajo and other tribes.

Resources at the **Zuni Archaeology Program Library** in Zuni cover Zuni prehistory, archaeology, history, and land use.

CAMPGROUNDS

You can find campsites at **Acoma Pueblo**, 50 miles west of Albuquerque; **Isleta Pueblo**, 8 miles southwest of Albuquerque; **Jemez Pueblo**, 44 miles north of Albuquerque; the **Jicarilla Apache Reservation**, Dulce; **Laguna Pueblo**, 45 miles west of Albuquerque; the **Mescalero Apache Reservation**, south central New Mexico; the **Navajo Reservation**, northwest New Mexico; **Santa Clara Pueblo**, 5 miles south of Espanola; and **Zuni Pueblo**, 40 miles south of Gallup.

NATIVE AMERICAN CENTERS

Organizations serving the Native American community in New Mexico include:

Albuquerque Indian Center, Albuquerque
Albuquerque Urban Indian Health Clinic, Albuquerque
Farmington Intertribal Indian Organization, Farmington
Gallup Friendship House, Gallup
Gallup Indian Community Center, Gallup
Indian Youth Council, Gallup.

CRAFT GUILDS AND COOPERATIVES

Crownpoint Rug Weavers' Association, Inc., in Crownpoint holds periodic Navajo rug auctions.

Eight Northern Pueblo Indian Artisans' Guild at San Juan Pueblo manufactures pottery, drums, jewelry, kachina dolls, and wood carvings.

INDIAN NEWSPAPERS AND NEWSLETTERS

There are many Native American newspapers and newsletters in New Mexico. They include: *The Apache Scout,* Mescalero Reservation, Mescalero; *Americans Before Columbus,* Albuquerque; *Bulletin,* Southern Pueblos Agency, Albuquerque; *Capital News,* Santo Domingo; *Cochiti Lake Sun,* Cochiti; *Distant Visions,* Institute of American Indian Art, Sante Fe; *Eight Northern Pueblos News,* San Juan Pueblo; *Indian Extension News,* New Mexico State University, Las Cruces; *Indian Forerunner,* San Juan Pueblo; *Jicarilla Chieftain,* Dulce; *The Messenger,* San Fidel; *Pueblo Horizon,* Indian Pueblo Cultural Center, Albuquerque; *Pueblo News,* Albuquerque; *Red Alert,* Albuquerque; *Red Times,* Laguna; *Tribal Peoples Survival Newsletter,* Albuquerque; *TSA' ASZI',* Pine Hill; *Zuni Carrier,* Zuni Pueblo, Zuni.

STATE AND REGIONAL ASSOCIATIONS

State and regional associations include:

Eight Northern Pueblos, Inc., San Juan Pueblo (P.O. Box 969, San Juan Pueblo 87566; 505-852-4265)
Five Sandoval Indian Pueblos, Inc., Bernalilo
Historical Society of New Mexico, Palace of the Governors, Santa Fe
Indian Advisory Commission, Albuquerque

New Mexico Indian Business Association, Albuquerque
New Mexico Indian Business Development Center, Albuquerque
New Mexico Office on Indian Affairs, Santa Fe
State Tribal Relations Committee, Albuquerque
Ten Southern Pueblos Council, Pueblo of Acoma, Acomita

TOURISM OFFICES

For general tourist information, contact the **New Mexico Department of Tourism** (P.O. Box 20003, Santa Fe 87503; 505-827-7400).

For local tourist information, contact the **Albuquerque Convention & Visitors Bureau** (P.O. Box 26866, Albuquerque 87125; 800-284-2282); the **Farmington Convention & Visitors Bureau** (203 West Main, Suite 401, Farmington 87401; 800-448-1240); the **Gallup Convention & Visitors Bureau** (P.O. Box 600, Gallup 87305; 800-242-4282); the **Portales Chamber of Commerce** (7th & Abilene, Portales 88130; 800-635-8036); the **Santa Fe Convention & Visitors Bureau** (P.O. Box 909, Santa Fe 87504; 800-777-CITY); or the **Taos County Chamber of Commerce** (P.O. Drawer 1, Taos 87571; 800-732-TAOS).

Selected Attractions:

NATIVE NEW MEXICO

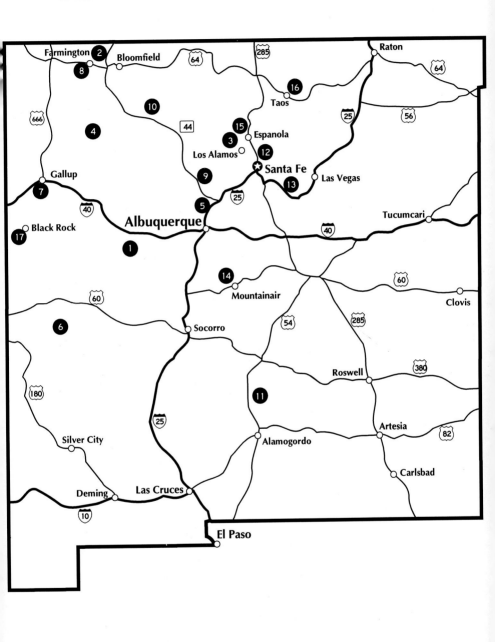

COLORADO

Sharks once swam in the seas that covered what we now call Colorado. The thought seems enigmatic in a state dominated by great mountain ranges. Yet it also encourages the traveler to consider the geological drama that transpired when great global plates shifted and forced their way toward the surface of the gigantic ocean.

Colorado gets its name from the Spanish. While it seems logical that "Colorado" might easily mean "the color red" when translated into English, that's not quite the case. *Roja* is the word for "red" in Spanish. However, with a bit of antiquated application, "Colorado" actually translates to mean "ruddy," or "reddish" in color.

Early Spanish explorers paddled and portaged their shallow boats about 100 miles up the 1400-mile length of the Colorado River, and anyone who has seen the Colorado River knows what a ruddy flowage it is. The Spanish were quick to claim the area, but they subsequently ignored it for the most part. This land of mountains and high plateaus was too rugged, too cost-inefficient, and too remote from the colonial settlements to the south.

Some anthropologists believe that Colorado's mountain ranges served as the only north-south bridge during the glacial ages. Those who subscribe to the "Bering Strait theory" of emigration between eastern Asia and the American continents during that epoch think it's possible that many of our hemisphere's first inhabitants literally walked across the spines of Colorado's mountains to their eventual homelands.

The Colorado area was ideally situated for such migrations, generation after generation, as peoples moved toward more hospitable climes. In fact, one might logically speculate that the great Mayan cultures of western South America may have developed many of their coping skills while trekking along the hostile track of the Rocky Mountains and other ranges.

Nonetheless, as time passed, the great mountain ranges of provided as much challenge to the "new" Native American people as they would thousands of years later for the incoming peoples from the south, the Spanish, and the east, the other Europeans. By then, the ice had melted. Great canyons and valleys had been formed. And most intimidating were the high-altitude peaks always surrounded by saw-toothed neighbors equally difficult to cross. It might be unfair to equate Colorado 2,000 years

---

Mesa Verde's Cliff Palace is one of the most spectacular ruins in Colorado.

ago with our picture today of Siberia or Mongolia, but if one considers the arduous distances, the heights, and the seasonal weather variations, there is rational evidence for the simple phrase: "It's a nice place to visit, but we wouldn't want to live here."

Today, the Ute are the only Native American people who live in the state. There are only two reservations in Colorado: the Southern Ute and the Ute Mountain reservations. The Southern Utes once considered what we now call Aspen their summer campgrounds; when the Spanish and Americans found gold and abundant furs abundant in the area, it assumed added value. For most travelers and explorers, however, the high mountain ranges were not bridges but walls impeding their progress westward or northward.

The wedding basket (above) and cradle board (right) are Ute creations.

CRADLEBOARD
Willow, deerskin

Ute - Southern Colo[rado]

Mitchell Indian Muse[um]

ANASAZI CULTURE

In the sections dealing with Arizona and New Mexico, we highlighted Canyon de Chelly and Chaco Canyon as central locations of the Anasazi culture—containing what the literate consider "prehistoric" relics of a past civilization. In Colorado there are at present two exceptional communities, one of which is nearing completion. Let us begin with what many consider the greatest cliff-dwelling community that has survived the elements, marauding bands of grave robbers, and the curiosity of the archaeologists and anthropologists: Mesa Verde.

What is called "Cliff Palace" was accidentally discovered by two cowboys—Robert Wetherill and Charlie Mason—on December 18, 1888, as they rode the mesa top looking for stray cattle. It was snowing, and they were concerned about the vagrant cattle, but as they approached the edge of the mesa they saw "a magnificent city" through the blowing snow. They were from the Mancos Valley to the east, and their curiosity led them to do some exploration. The two cowpokes brought a few artifacts back with them to prove that they had accomplished more than finding lost cattle.

The "magnificent city" of Cliff Palace was home to the Anasazi around 1200 A.D.

For the next 18 years, the two men guided individuals and groups through this marvelous ruin. Visitors camped nearby for days and weeks while exploring the site. At the time, there were no regulations governing invasions of the Native American past. As a result, many artifacts were taken as souvenirs, and graffiti and defacement took place. Finally, in 1909, the Smithsonian Institution pressured the federal government to halt such invasions and thefts. Archaeological experts tried to restore, insofar as was possible, the glory and grandeur of what was now called "Cliff Palace."

Set in a 78 million-year-old Cretaceous sandstone alcove created by a mixture of sandstone and slate that froze and expanded during cold and warm seasons, Cliff Palace had provided the Anasazi people with a natural roof for their habitation. In a sense, the cave was the original all-weather dwelling. Such gigantic in-cuts into cliff walls, placed above canyon floors and a sheer, treacherous climb below the mesa top, must have seemed safe from the elements, from hostile animals, and from other human beings.

We call the early inhabitants *Anasazi*, a Navajo word for "the ancient ones" or "the ancient foreigners." The Hopi, the Zuni, and other Pueblo people call them ancestors, and the significance of the people who lived on the mesa top beginning around 500 A.D. and moved seven centuries later to the cliff's protective alcoves is great. People still live in the Anasazi site at Canyon de Chelly; the Chaco Canyon ruins are sacred to many peoples; and Mesa Verde was a faraway but important Anasazi community. Together, these three formed what was a triad of productive, large communities perpetuating a classical culture.

Consider the Hopi Badger Clan, one of the four most important clans of this historical group. In his study of the Hopi, Frank Waters discovered that there were three divisions of the Badger Clan: Brown Badger, Grey Badger, and Black Badger. The Black Badger Clan was the original grouping, and when he let tribal elders speak, he realized that clan history was fading into transparent memory. His search for the Hopi's past ranged from Colorado to Mexico to New Mexico, where the "Narrow Hair Bang (Pueblo) People" lived in what is now San Felipe.

According to the Badger elders, the people finally "found a beautiful canyon and a huge cave in a cliff, in which they began to build houses and storerooms and kivas—a whole village." The village became so large and prosperous that the Butterfly Clan joined the Badger Clan, and other clans migrated to the area as well. Subsequently, there were problems with climate, seasonal changes, and population growth. People had difficulty surviving the lean years, and the clans had different opinions about the best way to survive. As a result, many moved elsewhere.

Waters was initially drawn to his studies of the Four Corners area through contact with Mesa Verde. He agreed with non-Indian archaeologists that a site called "Spruce Tree House," with its 114-rooms and eight-kiva structure, was most mysterious and important.

"I do not know where the ancient village of Salapa is," Hopi elder John Lansa told Waters, "with its spring and the spruce which grew out of the body of Salavi." Salavi was the Badger Clan's sacred leader, providing a sign that once identified the homeland. The clan had once sent messengers every year to honor the spirit, Salavi, symbolized by the spruce tree, and his final resting place, the village of Salapa.

Waters wondered if Spruce Tree House might relate to this aspect of Hopi history. He and his friend White Bear took Lansa, who had never been to Mesa Verde, to see if the site might hold significant indications of clan history. Sure enough, on Pictograph Point just down the canyon, was a set of drawings that depicted exactly what the Badger Clan had been preserving for centuries. Everything fit, from the figure of Salavi to the

Cliff Palace provided the Anasazi with a natural roof that protected them from the elements.

inclusion of the Butterfly Clan's symbol. Even the kivas were arranged in a pattern that replicates the footprint of the sacred badger. Further, the site presents documentation of disagreements between clans and their eventual separation and emigration to other places.

John Lansa was stunned by the revelations contained in the pictographs, but when he saw the great, ancient spruce tree at Mesa Verde, the pieces of the ancient tapestry all became stitched into living reality. After his death, Salavi had been transformed into a spruce tree. Here, without a doubt, was that spruce. Such is the immensity of the meaning and history of Mesa Verde, once home to 4,000 people.

• • •

We might turn now to America's "Pinto Bean Capital" in Dove Creek, Colorado, as the site of the next step in the myriad and colonial culture of the Anasazi. Contemporary locals and officials call this Montezuma Valley, one more misnomer when it comes to linking the present with the distant past.

The "Spruce Tree House" at Mesa Verde contains 114 rooms and 8 kivas.

Those who are captivated by the Anasazi or "prehistoric" civilization will be enthralled by the amazing discovery, in our own lifetime, of a place where an estimated 40,000 people lived between 800 and 1500 A.D. The folks who lived in the area of the Pinto Bean Capital and Montezuma Valley numbered ten times the people calling Mesa Verde their home.

A group called the Archaeological Conservancy believes this site to be the "largest, most extensive, underdeveloped archaeological resource in the United States." However, the Conservancy advocates "limited development," also the current position of the National Parks and Conservation Association. These two groups plus an amalgam of other groups, both Native American and non-Indian, have conceptualized an entirely new kind of national, historical park.

There is a thirty-mile corridor that creates what is called, in contemporary terms, a megalopolis, but is actually a series of pueblos. Each had thousands of rooms, hundreds of kivas, numerous towers, and vast peripheral suburbs. Take "Yellowjacket," for example, where the experts believe there are as many as 2,000 rooms, 128 kivas, 28 towers, and a Great Kiva. Some believe there are astrological aspects to the site as well, but the

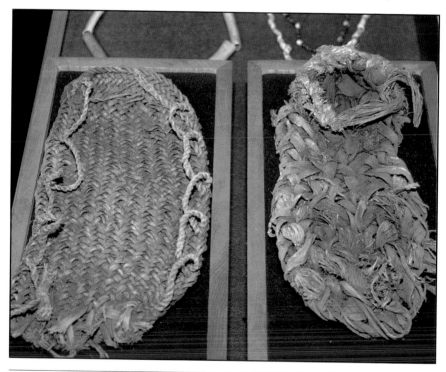

Sandals such as these were worn by Colorado's Anasazi.

"Stonehenge" syndrome can be misapplied even to such developed civilizations. It must be noted that this area is far from the Central and South American cultures, where such science and literacy was prevalent.

A great drought occurred between 1266 and 1300, one so intense that it is easy to verify through modern agricultural and geological science. This was not an isolated geographic event. The entire demography of the Plains Indians changed during this horrendous, 34-year period of natural and environmental deprivation. The people retreated to areas where they found water, game, and a perpetuation of life even in the toughest of times. For the peoples of the Four Corners area, this period was the toughest of times.

Dr. William Lipe of Washington State University also directs the Crow Canyon Archaeological Center in Colorado. Of all the groups studying Montezuma Valley's early history, the scholars under Lipe's direction are at the forefront. In *National Parks*, the publication of the National Parks and Conservation Association, Prof. Lipe writes: "Anasazi history is valuable in and of itself, as a unique thread, but it has a lot to teach us about how all of us developed. Their history is a microcosm of cultural

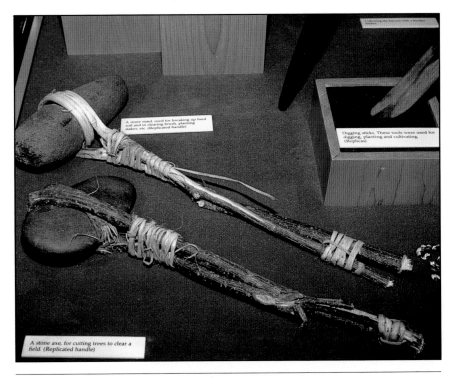

Tools and other artifacts on display at the Anasazi Heritage Center in Dolores, CO.

change found all over the world, because most cultures progressed from small farming to long-term sustainable social organizations." This progression, according to Lipe, was happening when the Montezuma Valley Anasazi culture was forced to vacate the area.

What is unique in Dove Creek-Montezuma Valley area is the fact that both Native American and non-Indian experts are being cautious about both their conclusions and their explorations. This is a trend that is to be endorsed and applauded. As we have noted in the Arizona and New Mexico sections, many sites now covered by the dust and sand of centuries will not be violated. They will be left alone, for early expeditions have revealed the generic nature of each place. The public is allowed to witness enough of the past to be inspired, and selected areas are scientifically examined, but for the most part the past is treated with respect and reverence. It is left intact.

Montezuma Valley is part of this enlightened educational environment. It will not be swept clean with a new broom. The scholars and experts will, no doubt, violate some Native American peoples' concerns about excavation or resurrection of earlier generations. However, 88 percent of the ruins

The Escalante Ruin is part of the Anasazi Heritage Center.

here will remain untouched. At Mesa Verde, one archaeologist notes, "They excavated everything." At Chaco Canyon the valuable crossbeams, or "vigas," were burned as firewood—no one knew about carbon tree-ring dating in the first decades of the 20th century.

At Montezuma Valley, the scientists are utilizing every known technical advance, from satellite images to pollen analysis, plus such methodologies as Carbon-14 dating and "archaeomagnetism," which examines fire rings by utilizing the iron found in the rocks and the changes of polar magnetism, so the fires can be "dated." Then there is the computer, which can create models that analyze environmental changes and population fluctuations.

Enter the Bureau of Land Management, the giant federal bureaucracy that controls use of lands that "nobody wants." The BLM has enabled the parks people not only to set aside a dozen sites that will be incorporated into a park, but they have denied public or private access to these places. In Montezuma Valley there will be, for example, only one public park. There has been opposition to the park's creation, but projections indicate that the Anasazi National Historical Park will add more than $90 million to the local economy, in addition to 200 or more jobs.

At this writing, nothing definitive has been determined regarding the completion of or access to this exceptional park. However, travelers can contact the Park Service or the Colorado section of the BLM for a progress report concerning the project. There is also an office for what has been called "The Dolores Project," another name for the Anasazi Heritage Center or Monument, which may be contacted regarding progress on the park (see listings at the end of this chapter).

Arapaho Culture

Before considering the two Ute Reservations in Colorado, we must consider two other tribal nations that called the area home for many centuries. The Southern Arapaho people settled near Colorado's Arkansas River. The group called itself *Inuana-ina*, or "the people," as did so many others. While rival tribes called them less complimentary names, the Pawnee dubbed them Arapaho, or "trader," which is not too far from the Kiowa's word for them, *Ahyato*. These are Algonquin-speaking people, relatively rare in the far west. As such, they are probably related to the other Algonquin-language-based Blackfoot, Cheyenne and Gros Ventre. Some believe their origins to have been in what is now Minnesota and

Saskatchewan.

The Arapaho are a Plains Indian nation. Their culture, both for hunting and war, came to center upon horses and horsemanship as they adapted to the great ocean of grasslands. They went where the buffalo migrated, packing up their skin tipis and migrating to the next hunting ground. However, the basic similarity between the Arapaho and other Plains Indians involved three elements: the Sun Dance, the medicine bundle, and military clans or societies. The clans were like grades in a school, for the Arapaho had eight secret military societies into which boys, adolescents, and then men graduated. The medicine bundle custom involved vision quests and societal collections of sacred elements. For the Arapaho, the most sacrosanct was a carefully preserved pipe that was smoked only at special times with special rituals. The Arapaho also kept a sacred hoop. Even the crafts the women created—beadwork, clothing, tipi coverings—told the various stories of the "Inuna-ina."

The Sun Dance, which emerges with varying degrees of power and animosity, was the essential ceremony of the Arapaho, and of many Plains peoples. There is no contemporary equivalent in today's non-Indian society, but if one were to combine Thanksgiving with Christmas and Easter celebrations, including all the perpetual and eternal symbolism, one might arrive at a celebration of approximately equal spiritual power and meaning. The Arapaho followed the tradition of the Sun Dance, celebrating when natural fruits and berries ripened, and it was a time of testing personal, spiritual, and physical endurance.

Historically, the Arapaho fought to preserve their heritage and their holdings. They joined forces with the Cheyenne, the Comanches, and the Kiowas. What is important to note is that the Arapaho were, as result of the Medicine Lodge Treaty of 1867, forced to move from their homeland to "Indian Territory" along with the Southern Cheyenne. One year later, they were told to move to Pine Ridge in South Dakota. When another move was proposed in 1876, they balked, especially the northern Arapaho. The federal government then persuaded the northern Shoshone to accept the Arapaho presence in Wyoming, in the Wind River Reservation.

One decade later, the Arapahos helped create another federal dilemma, for they became very involved with what is called the "Ghost Dance Religion," along with the Paiute and the Sioux. Today the descendants of the northern and southern Arapaho tribes either live on the Wind River

Reservation in Wyoming or within the various communities of Oklahoma.

CHEYENNE CULTURE

The Sioux gave them the name "Cheyenne," but the people called themselves *Tsistsistas*, or "beautiful people." For the Sioux, "Cheyenne" simply meant "those who speak a different language," a generous and peaceful description.

The Cheyenne emigrated from the upper midwest—it is documented that the first time these people met Europeans was in 1680, when they spent time with La Salle at his fort in Illinois. Their trek took them to the Missouri River, where they continued their agricultural practices. They soon learned about horses and, as their own history says, "They lost the corn." One authority even notes that in the late 1700s, the Cheyenne stopped making pottery, mainly because it did not travel well.

The Cheyenne became a classical Plains Indians group. They established ten mobile bands. The Sioux pushed them in one direction and others pushed them elsewhere, but the Cheyenne also did some relocating

A diorama depicting Cheyenne life in Colorado.

of other tribes, such as the Kiowa. About 1330, the people split into two groups, one heading north and the other going south. The southern Cheyenne, like the Arapaho, chose to live on the banks and watershed of the Arkansas River in eastern Colorado.

At first the Cheyenne fought the Kiowas and the Comanches, but eventually, in about 1840, the three groups banded together to battle a multitude of tribes: the Apache, the Crow, the Shoshone, the Pawnee, and the Utes.

The Cheyenne called the Sun Dance the "New Life Lodge," and they organized themselves into a very sophisticated and complex governmental system known as "The Council of Forty-Four." The tribe's military societies were, for all intents and purposes, similar to divisions of the U.S. military, each having its own codes and specialties. There were the Societies of the Dog, Fox, Shield, Wolf, Elk, "Northern Crazy Dogs," Bowstrings or "Contraries," and the "Hotamitanio," or Dog Soldiers. This last society would wage life-and-death conflicts with the United States government.

Above all, or so it seems, the Cheyenne wanted to maintain peace with the non-Indians who were moving into their territory. In 1825, they signed a treaty. In 1851, the Cheyenne were part of two treaties signed at Ft. Laramie in Wyoming. The westward-moving Americans obviously wanted a safe passage from the Mississippi to the western coast. The Cheyenne granted that passage, but wherever they turned, the migrants and freebooters took advantage of the freedom to move through Cheyenne country. Prospectors, land agents, railroad dealers, ranchers, territorial governments—all figured that what was safe was also exploitable.

In 1857, as the southern Cheyenne's defense of their land and treaty rights resulted in armed conflict, the U.S. Army attacked. In 1858, the gold rush to Pike's Peak ensued, bringing many more armed men to fight the Cheyenne and others who stood in the way of prospective wealth. The governor of the Colorado Territory wanted to open up the Arapaho and Cheyenne lands to settlement as soon as possible. The tribe refused to sell or deal with interlopers. They had treaties in their possession.

Although American history has witnessed many "forced marches" and relocations, there is no single incident more symbolic of the plight of the Native American than the 1865 disaster at Sand Creek, Colorado. Quite simply, it was an unjustified genocide unequaled in American history.

The story: Beginning in 1864, Col. John Chivington and his troop of volunteers waged war against the Cheyenne and the Arapaho in the Colorado Territory. Chivington borrowed a page out of Sherman's burn, pillage, rape, and loot campaign in Atlanta, Georgia, a kind of violence thought to be the only way of dealing with desperate enemies. Some books call this conflict the Cheyenne-Arapaho War or the Colorado War.

The Cheyenne had already signed numerous treaties and vowed to remain peaceful. Black Kettle was a southern Cheyenne, and he led 600 people, including some southern Arapaho, to a safe location on the banks of the Arkansas River. His peaceful declarations were widespread. Black Kettle wanted peace. He wanted to preserve his people.

Chivington, on the other hand, was a subscriber to the genocide theory prevalent at the time in the West: "The only good Indian is a dead Indian." He sent his voluntary cavalry and artillery men, self-proclaimed "Hundred Dazers" who served short enlistment periods. They shot and burned out anybody and everybody—mostly old men, women, and children. Two hundred people were killed beneath Chief Black Kettle's white flag, which flew above the U.S. flag on the pole of his tipi.

There is no national monument to this tragedy, save a roadside marker and a dot on some maps near the junction of a dry creek bed and Cty. Hwy. 96, halfway between the two small towns of Brandon and Chivington. The site is about 20 miles downstream from the town called Kit Carson, named after another western figure noted for his cruel treatment of the Native American people of the Southwest.

The incident at Sand Creek more or less precipitated the eventual departure of the southern Cheyenne from their Colorado homeland, along with the Arapaho. These groups joined other Plains Indians in their fight against incoming troops and settlers. Between 1866 and 1868, Gen. Winfield Scott Hancock chose to pit his military strength against two southern Cheyenne groups headed by Chiefs Tall Bull and White Horse. Among Hancock's corps of officers was George Armstrong Custer. The Hancock campaign was unsuccessful.

Custer, though, encountered Black Kettle in November of 1868. Despite Sand Creek, the Cheyenne chief almost inexplicably maintained a truce with the U.S. government, and had retreated to the Washita River in Indian Territory (now Oklahoma). Custer's troops attacked his band again, and this time Black Kettle and about 100 of his people died, once again beneath the white flag. Other pockets of Cheyenne would not be so pacific. They fought on in places like Summit Springs in Colorado, only to be vanquished.

The northern Cheyenne also continued their battles against encroachment, and undoubtedly more than a small degree of revenge was involved when they joined the War of the Black Hills, which included the skirmish at Little Bighorn in 1876. This famous battle brought the military career of George Armstrong Custer to a violent and ignominious end.

The Battle of Dull Knife, named after a great northern Cheyenne war chief, essentially concluded the Black Hills conflict. Dull Knife led a force of 300 northward, pushed by 13,000 troops, militia, and armed settlers. The northern Cheyenne surrendered at the Pine Ridge Sioux Reservation in South Dakota and were eventually given their own land in Lame Deer, Montana. The southern Cheyenne were allowed to share land with the southern Arapaho in Oklahoma.

Like the Arapaho, the Cheyenne have been displaced from Colorado. Yet their history is as important as any other Native American nation that fought to keep what it considered its place in the universe. The Cheyenne were not a warlike, bellicose people. They were deeply religious, and their culture in the area was enlivened by rich ceremony, humor, dance, and historic portrayals.

If there is a sadness outside of the truth reflected in Colorado's history, it is that Colorado pays abundant tribute through place-names to both the Arapaho and the southern Cheyenne that once dominated the eastern slopes of the Colorado Rockies. Those place-names are about all that is left of these proud and courageous people in their ancestral homeland.

UTE CULTURE

A traveler who visits Aspen, Colorado, in the summertime will instantly understand why the group called "Ute," described themselves as the people "high up," or the people living in "the land of the sun." At one time, the Ute ruled the Rockies, from the waters of the San Juan River in the south to the Sevier River in what is now Utah and all the way to the Wyoming gap in the range.

The Ute—of which there were seven primary bands—were not part of the Plains or the Colorado Plateau peoples. These mountain dwellers lived in what anthro-geographers call the "Great Basin Culture Area." So dominant were they that their language was termed "Uto-Aztecan," and it included the languages of the Shoshone and the Paiute people. What the "Basin" basically includes is the area between the Rocky Mountain and

Sierra Nevada ranges. Some called them "Digger Indians" because they often had to dig into the dry land of the basin for food and water.

The Ute people were, in fact, primarily hunters rather than gatherers. The western spine of the continent, the Continental Divide, provided them with ample resources that were denied their cellar-floor brethren. A marvelous cornucopia was theirs to harvest, but they also had to endure tough climatic changes. The Ute lay claim to the western slope, a region that offered rain, snow, and unpredictable changes in climate.

In the early epochs, the Ute consisted of small bands of families and clans. Among the most honored within each band were those artisans who could chip an amazing range of arrow and spear points. Because of their exquisite hunting skills, the Ute supplied the "flatland" Pueblo peoples (and subsequently the Spanish) with pelts and game. In exchange, the Ute picked up agricultural skills, but they ultimately found their future in the horse.

The Ute adapted quickly to the culture of the horse and all the implicit changes involved. They became "ranchers" of a sort, for they controlled the vast grassland parks that are found throughout the high ranges.

These moccasins are typical of Ute footwear design.

They controlled the spaces where horses could graze during a significant portion of each year. Their horses never lacked water or food. While the Ute basically conquered, contained, and maintained the side of the mountain ranges whose rivers flowed toward the Pacific Ocean, they occasionally ventured over the eastern slopes—mainly to keep tribes like the Arapaho from flowing through the valleys between the 14,000-foot peaks and into their own lush homeland.

When the trouble came to the Ute, it came in the form of paper treaties insisted upon by men wearing miners' hats and the blue tunics of the U.S. Cavalry. Suddenly, Ute superiority, territorial claims, and defenses were in jeopardy. The Ute signed many of their rights away in treaties concluded before the Civil War, but by 1876, when Colorado achieved statehood and adopted "Centennial State," as its nickname, the mining industry had begun making inroads.

"The Utes Must Go" became a sociopolitical rallying cry—despite the Utes' willingness to help incoming people find the motherlodes and to fight against the Navajo and the Apache. One of the greatest of contemporary Ute chiefs was Ouray—after whom one of Colorado's most beautiful mountain towns is named—who spoke both Spanish and English, as well as several other languages of the people of the region. Kit Carson considered Chief Ouray one of the most impressive men he had ever encountered.

In 1879, conflicts arose between the a Ute group and a missionary/Indian agent who tried to convert the Utes to his religion and the European way of farming. The change in farming methods would have entailed plowing under the group's traditional pastures. The disagreement led to violence, and people on both sides of the issue died, including the agent and his family. It was not one of the brightest hours for the people who lived in the land of the sun.

Generals Sherman and Sheridan, who were assigned to command the entire western region of the country following the Civil War, sought to wipe out the enemy. Thankfully, though, Carl Schurz, a native German, a lawyer from Milwaukee, and a Civil War general who had campaigned vigorously for President Abraham Lincoln, intervened. Schurz opposed the conflict proposed by the more prestigious generals. Instead of approving the order, he sent John Quincy Adams' son, Charles Adams, a noted diplomat and negotiator, to meet with the Utes.

Adams met with Chief Ouray, and positive results included negotiated hostage releases and guarantees of freedom and non-retribution. Unfortunately, Ouray died one year later, in 1880, at the age of 46. His death marked the move of the White River Utes.

Today there are three Ute reservations, two in Colorado and one in Utah. In Colorado, the Southern Ute Reservation is located at one edge of the Mesa Verde National Park. Near Ignacio, Colorado, this reservation includes the Mouache and Capote Ute bands. The other Ute land in the state is the Ute Mountain Reservation, located near Towaoc, Colorado. This group holds parcels of land in New Mexico and Utah as well, and the reservation is home to the Wimnuche band. The Uintah and Ouray Reservation is located near Ft. Duchesne, Utah, and is considered the inheritance of Chief Ouray's White River Ute people.

CONCLUSION

Considering the extensive history of Native Americans in Colorado, the native presence in the state is slight. In part, this minimal habitation is due to the unmitigated violence of earlier days, fueled by the rush for the gold and silver that was thought to permeate the entire Rocky

Petroglyphs at Kiva Point include butterfly and Venus Clan symbols.

Mountain chain. The forced migration of the native peoples was in no small part aided by the unrelenting military persecution engineered by figures including Generals Sherman and Sheridan, George Armstrong Custer, Kit Carson, John Chivington, and others.

Colorado played a distinctive role in the movement of native peoples from all directions, but today is virtually bereft of its Native American heritage. However, the ruins at Mesa Verde and the evolving Anasazi Heritage Center provide the traveler with an abundance of clues revealing how significant the Colorado area has been to our Native American fellow-citizens. A visit to Mesa Verde can also help the traveler understand that a self-sufficient, self-defined culture once lived and prospered here.

Some years ago, when I was a young person visiting Mesa Verde, a park ranger spoke to our group around a blazing, mesquite fire. We had spent the day wandering through the multitude of ruins, and the ranger was sharing his perceptions of the area's original inhabitants. The warmth of the circle and the paternal tone of the narration almost put me to sleep, but a final story, which seems to contradict what is now known about the Anasazi, nonetheless caught my attention. True or not, the story makes a point about native cultural integrity.

"Let me tell you about one of our most interesting discoveries," the ranger said. "We have found that the people here traded goods for Spanish blankets or robes made of wool. But the people of Mesa Verde did not simply don these robes or put the blankets on their beds.

"The people of Mesa Verde took the Spanish cloth, but the women took each bolt or blanket apart, thread by thread. Imagine undoing thousands of small woolen threads and carefully preserving them on spools and bobbins."

Why? We all wondered in the dying light above Mesa Verde's monumental ruins.

"Why? Because it wasn't theirs. The designs were Spanish or Mexican. The weaving, the patterns, and the spiritual signature were not theirs. So the people who lived here chose to take the resources of a strange culture that they did not know or understand and, thread by thread, took the fabric apart and reassembled it into something they knew to be theirs. Their symbols, their labor, their prayers, their uses, their integrity, and their own creations emerged from that Spanish wool."

MUSEUMS, ARCHIVES, AND CULTURAL CENTERS

Aguilar Museum (137 Main St., Aguilar) is open by appointment, and has displays of local history and Southwestern artifacts.

Anasazi Heritage Center Museum, located two miles west of Dolores on Highway 184, features major ruins and exhibits on the Anasazi culture. Open year-round, 9 a.m. to 5 p.m. Admission is free.

Aultman Museum (136 E. Main St., Trinidad) features 100 years of black and white photography in Trinidad and Las Animas County. Open from Memorial Day through Labor Day, Monday through Saturday, 10:00 to 4:00.

Canon City Municipal Museum (6th and Royal Gorge Blvd., Canon City) has exhibits on Dall DeWeese, a nationally known hunter, and on gemstones and Indian artifacts. Admission is charged.

Charles Eagle Plume Trading Post, located 10 miles east of Estes Park on Highway 7, houses an exceptional collection of Indian artifacts. Open from 9:00 to 5:00 daily from Memorial Day through Labor Day. Admission is free.

Colorado History Museum (1300 Broadway, Denver) has ethnological and photographic collections of Plains and Southwest Indians.

A view of Spruce Tree House in Mesa Verde.

155

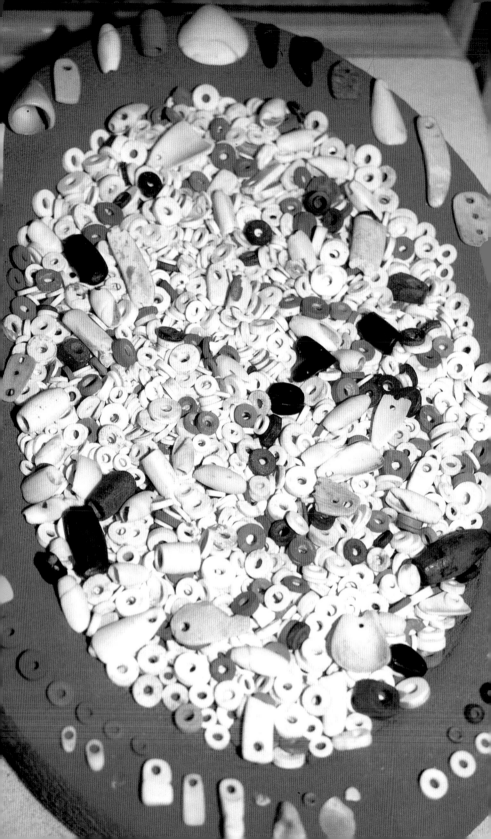

Crow Canyon Archaeological Center (2390 County Rd. K, Cortez) is archaeological research and education facility. The center offers day- and week-long programs in Southwestern history and archaeological digs, and reservations are required to visit. Admission is charged.

Denver Art Museum (100 W. 14th Ave. Parkway, Denver) includes North American Indian art, traditional clothing, Navajo and Pueblo pottery, and Hopi kachina dolls.

Denver Museum of Natural History (City Park, Denver) features the Hall of Prehistoric People of the Americas and a collection of Paleo-Indian specimens.

El Pueblo Museum (905 S. Prairie, Pueblo) is located on a site that was once a crossroad for Ute, Cheyenne, Arapaho and Kiowa Indians. Open year-round, Tuesday through Saturday, 10 to 3. Admission is charged.

Fort Collins Museum (200 Mathews St., Fort Collins) houses displays including Pre-Columbian and Plains Indian artifacts. The museum contains two historic cabins and a one-room schoolhouse preserved from their original sites. Open Tuesday through Saturday, 10 to 5; Sunday, 1 to 5. Admission is free.

Fort Uncompahgre Living History Museum shows what life was like for trappers and traders in the 1840s. Open Tuesday through Sunday from 10:00 to 5:00. Admission is charged.

Heritage Museum (430 W. Main, Hotchkiss) offers a variety of contemporary and historical exhibits, as well as rotating art shows. Open Memorial Day through Labor Day from 9 to 5. Admission is charged.

Historic Museum and Institute of Western Colorado (4th and Ute, Grand Junction) includes the Ute Indian Collection and Teller Indian School Collection of basketry, artifacts, manuscripts, and photographs.

Kiowa County Museum (1313 Main St., Cuchara) includes relics of the past and exhibits on local history. Open May 30 through September 10, from 1 to 5. Admission is free.

Koshare Indian Kiva Museum (115 W. 18th St., La Junta) has a nationally recognized collection of Native American art and artifacts. Koshare Indian dancers perform from June through August. Admission is charged.

Leanin' Tree Museum of Western Art (6055 Longbow Dr., Boulder) features one of the most extensive collections of contemporary Western art. Open Monday through Friday, 8 to 4:30, year-round. Admission is free.

Anasazi beads displayed at Mesa Verde.

Louden-Henritze Archaeology Museum, at Trinidad State Junior College, houses exhibits including geological and archaeological dioramas, fossils, and arrowheads.

Luther E. Bear and E.S. Museums (Richardson Hall, Adams State College, Alamosa) exhibits Pueblo Indian cultural artifacts, primarily pottery and Navajo weaving.

Manitou Cliff Dwellings Museum (west of Manitou Springs on Highway 24) features dwellings of Anasazi Indians, circa 1100 to 1300 A.D. Open June through August, 10 to 5. Admission is charged.

Robbers Roost Western Museum (6001 Boulder, Rye) has displays of guns and Indian items. Open May through September, 10 to 4. Admission is free.

Salida Museum (406 W. Rainbow Blvd., Salida) displays Indian, pioneer, and railroad artifacts. Open May through September, 11 to 7. Admission is free.

Sky Ute Gallery Museum and the **Southern Ute Indian Cultural Center** (P.O. Box 737, Ignacio) feature works by Southern Ute artists and craftsmen.

Taylor Museum for Southwestern Studies at the Colorado Springs Fine Arts Center (30 W. Dale St, Colorado Springs) offers exhibits of Native American arts, including Navajo rugs and blankets, Pueblo woven textiles, baskets and pottery, Zuni fetishes, Mimbres bowls, kachinas, and jewelry.

University of Colorado Center and Cultural Park (downtown Cortez) provides information on archaeological sites, tours, and evening programs that feature Indian storytellers and presentations of Indian culture.

Ute Indian Museum (17253 Chipeta Dr., Montrose), located on site of Chief Ouray's 400-acre farm, reveals the history of Utes through dioramas, photographs, and maps. The museum's Annual Native American Lifeways exhibit is a free cultural fair featuring demonstrations and exhibits of Native American arts, crafts, and cuisine.

MONUMENTS, HISTORIC SITES, AND PARKS

Bent's Old Fort National Historic Site (off Highway 194, La Junta) includes a reconstructed trading post that was once the hub for American trade into Mexico. An 1840 Indian Encampment is located in the cottonwood grove near the Old Fort.

Bent's Old Fort recreates life in the Old West around 1840.

Chimney Rock Archaeological Area (south of Highway 160, between Durango and Pagosa Springs), features unique rock spires marking the northernmost limits of the Chacoan Empire. The site offers free tours from May through September.

Comanche National Grasslands (Highways 350 and 160, La Junta) features more than 400,000 acres of range lands, home to 275 species of birds and 40 species of mammals.

The **Curecant National Recreation Area** (nine miles west of Gunnison on Highway 50) consists of three connecting lakes—Blue Mesa, Morrow Point, and Crystal—surrounded by mesa country.

Empire Valley Ute Indian Campground, located at the Union Pass scenic overlook, features gold mining camp cottages, historic Minton Park, and the Miners' Cemetery.

Escalante Ruins (overlooking the McPhee Reservoir near Dolores) is a site that was once inhabited by the Anasazi. Admission is free.

Four Corners Area Monument (near Cortez, on the Ute Mountain and Navajo Indian Reservations), is the only place where the corners of all four states meet. Open year-round; admission is free.

Greenhorn Meadows Park (Highway 165 in Colorado City) includes a historic marker that commemorates the battle between Comanche Chief Cuerno Verde and Spanish explorer Juan Bautista de Anza in 1779. Admission is free; there is a fee for camping.

Greenhorn Mountain (Highway 165, Rye) features a 12,349-foot peak named for Comanche Chief Cuerno Verde, killed in battle near the mountain's base in 1779. Admission is free.

Hovenweep National Monument (40 miles west of Cortez), features Anasazi ruins with square, oval, circular, and D-shaped towers. Open year-round; admission is free. Also listed under Utah.

Lowry Indian Ruins is one of the largest and best preserved painted Anasazi kivas in the world. It's located 26 miles north of Cortez on Highway 666. At Pleasant View, turn left and continue nine miles. Admission is free.

Mesa Verde National Park (nine miles east of Cortez on Highway 160) features cliff-side dwellings and other ruins of the Anasazi culture. Admission is free.

Mount Blanca (western Huerfano Valley, Walsenburg) was considered "the Sacred Mountain of the East" by Indian groups. Admission is free.

Pike's Stockade (four miles east of Stanford on River Rd.) is a reconstruction of Zebulon Pike's outpost in the San Luis Valley, established in

1807. Open Memorial Day through Labor Day, 9 to 5; admission is free.

Rendezvous of Cultures (Fort Garland) shows an authentic gathering of the Hispanic, Indian and military influences during the mid- to late-1800s in the San Luis Valley. Admission is charged.

Sharp's Trading Post (Highway 69 west of Gardner) is a two-story adobe building that served as a hotel and trading post on the road to Mosca Pass. Admission is free.

Unaweep/Tabeguache Scenic and Historic Byway is a 138-mile route that follows Highways 141 and 145 from outside Grand Junction to Placerville.

Ute Mountain Tribal Park (just south of Mesa Verde, near Towaoc) encompasses 125,000 acres of wilderness, with hundreds of Anasazi ruins and historic Ute rock art sites. Full day tours, backpacking, camping, and day hiking tours are given. Call (303) 565-8548 for information.

Weminuche Wilderness Area (northeast of Durango) is the state's largest wilderness area, encompassing one-half million acres of rugged high country. There is a fee for camping.

CALENDAR OF EVENTS

JANUARY
- The **Meeker Massacre Sled Dog Classic** takes place in Meeker.

FEBRUARY
- The **Tri-State Art Show** takes place in Yuma in February. Call the West Yuma County Chamber, (303) 848-2704, for information.

MARCH
- The **Denver March Pow Wow**, in Denver, brings together dancers from 70 tribes and 22 states.
- **Monte Vista Crane Festival** is held in Monte Vista in March.
- In Springfield, the **Spring Equinox Festival** celebrates the arrival of spring.
- Late in the month, the **Bear Dance** and **Spring Welcome** take place in Ignacio and Towaoc.

MAY
- The **Bear Dance** is performed late in the month on the Southern Ute Reservation.

JUNE

- Early in the month, the **Bear Dance** is held at Ute Mountain, Towaoc.

JULY

- Late in the month, the **Sun Dance** is performed at the Southern Ute Reservation.

SEPTEMBER

- At mid-month, the **Native American Lifeways Festival** is held in Montrose. Call 800-873-0244 for information.
- On the third weekend of the month, an **Indian Rodeo** is held in Ignacio. A **Tribal Fair** and **Dances** take place at the Southern Ute Reservation.
- The **Annual Rock Art Celebration**, a free event including music, dance, and outdoor theater, is held in Rangely. Call the Rangely Area Chamber of Commerce, (303) 675-5290, for information.

CAMPGROUNDS

Campsites in Colorado include: the **Navajo Site Recreation Area**, located at Navajo Reservoir, two miles south of Arboles, on County Rd. 982; the **Santa Clara Pueblo**, 5 miles south of Espanola; the **Southern Ute Reservation**, in southwestern Colorado; and the **Zuni Pueblo**, 40 miles south of Gallup.

CRAFT GUILDS

Ute Mountain Ute Pottery (12 miles south of Cortez, in Towaoc) features handmade pots unique to the Ute Mountain tribe. Open Monday through Saturday year-round, and Sundays in summer. Call (303) 565-8548 for information.

NATIVE AMERICAN CENTERS

Centers serving Native Americans in Colorado include:
Denver Indian Center, 4407 Morrison Rd., Denver 80219; (303) 937-1005
Eagle Lodge, 2801 E. Colfax #201, Denver 80206; (303) 764-0036.
Native American Fish & Wildlife Society, 750 Burbank, Broomfield 80020; (303) 466-1725.

Native American Rights Fund, 1506 Broadway, Boulder 80302; (303) 447-8760.

INDIAN NEWSLETTERS

Native American publications include: the newsletter of **Denver Native Americans United**, Denver; *Guts & Tripe*, Coalition of American Indian Citizens, Denver; the *Indian Times*, Denver; the newsletter of the **National Indian Health Board**, Denver; the newsletter of the **Native American Rights Fund**, Boulder; and *Rising Up*, published by the Indian Awareness Group in Englewood.

STATE AND REGIONAL AGENCIES

Agencies dealing with Native American affairs include:

Colorado Commission on Indian Affairs in Denver, which works to improve the relationship between the government and the Indian people of Colorado.

Colorado Indian Employment Assistance Center, in Denver, which provides job-hunting assistance.

TOURISM OFFICES

The **Colorado Indian Chamber of Commerce** (930 W. 7th Ave., Denver 80204; 303-220-9747) promotes Native American enterprises.

The **Southern Ute Tourist Center/Ignacio Chamber** (P.O. Box 737, Ignacio 81137; 800-876-7017) offers information on tourist attractions in the Ignacio area.

Selected Attractions:

NATIVE COLORADO

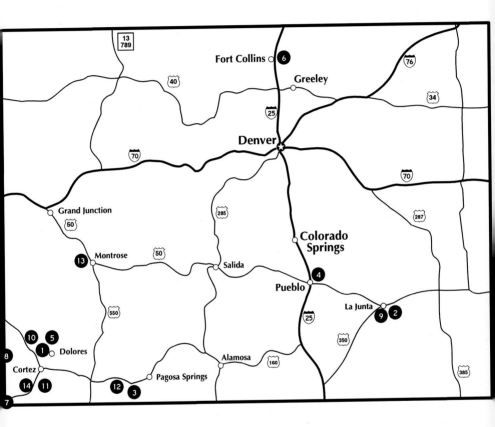

UTAH

INTRODUCTION

A number of states were named after Native American references to rivers, lakes, and geography. A few were named after the Indian population in residence when non-Indian settlers arrived—the Dakotas, Illinois, Indiana, and Utah.

The Ute people may not have been the first tribal group to consider the Utah area its homeland, but they were there when pioneers crossed the Rockies. Ute Pass in Colorado was once a main passage for the Ute people who crossed from eastern to western slopes. Many were headed toward the place we now call Utah.

The Ute did not welcome the newcomers with open arms. The region is among America's most varied in terms of topography and climate, and it makes many demands of all who choose to reside there. The so-called Colorado Plateau is what we generally consider the Four Corners area today, and southern Utah formed the fourth corner. Today, that sector also includes what is considered the largest Native American habitation in Utah, a portion of the Navajo Nation.

Yet that is not the only dimension to Utah's role in Native American history. The area also included what is now called the "Desert Culture Core Area." What we now consider to be the Great Basin, existing from about 9000 B.C. until 1000 B.C., had its own "primitive" tribal groups that foraged throughout the area to harvest or to take what might be useful or edible.

During the final stages of the Pleistocene Era, as the glaciers slowly melted and retreated toward the north, a great sea known as the Bonneville Lake was left in the glacial wake. We've heard and seen contemporary automotive speed records set in the Bonneville Flats, but what remains of the primeval salted sea is in fact the Great Salt Lake. Native Americans once controlling the area also controlled the commercial value of its salt: salt for hides, salt for food, salt for sovereignty.

The earliest examples of basketry on our continent are found in Utah at a site called Danger Cave, located not far from the salt flats. The Indians who mined the salt from the barren land traded it for sustaining grains, and for reeds with which the baskets were woven. For those who

Newspaper Rock, in the Canyonland area, contains some of the most vivid and vibrant rock art in the Southwest.

learned of its preservative value and its ability to enhance flavor, salt was a resource worthy of protecting. The latter-day Utes were among those groups that did not hesitate to protect their territorial rights.

ANASAZI COLONIES

Hovenweep National Monument in Utah may be the northernmost Anasazi outpost. Archaeologists and anthropologists are not certain when the Hovenweep—a Ute term meaning "deserted valley"—area was settled, but they estimate that Anasazi or pueblo farming began in the San Juan River Valley about 2,000 years ago.

Hovenweep is at the northern edge of the civilization inhabited by the "Colorado Plateau" peoples. Evidence indicates that Hovenweep was a colonial outpost of the Anasazi culture.

Like many western "monuments" to past cultures, Hovenweep is not easy to reach, but once there, the reward is generous. The traveler can venture south from Moab, Utah, on U.S. 191, west from Cortez, Colorado, on U.S. 666, or south from the Monument Valley region where U.S. 163 meets U.S. 191.

There is a paved road that goes to Hatch, a trading post, and extends about 16 miles to the major ruins of "Square Tower," where there is also a campground. Coming south from U.S. 666, to find the "Lowry Ruin," the traveler may encounter the seasonal risk of mud-soaked and impassable roads, as well as on the stretch of unpaved road between the Ismay Trading Post and the oblique turn-off to the Hatch Trading Post. If you reach Aneth, Utah, you have missed the variety of access points.

If there is a key element of interest, it lies in the fact that the people of Hovenweep, like so many other Anasazi or early pueblo people, left the security of their superior architecture and agriculture for alternative settlement at about the same time that so many others did—around 1300 A.D.

There is a U.S. ranger station at the site, but that's about all that is available to the curious, potential camper. All other supplies, including firewood, are available at one of the trading posts. If you wish to stay elsewhere overnight and visit the site during daylight hours, motels are located in Blanding or Bluff, Utah, or in Cortez, Colorado.

What is to be learned at Hovenweep? There is the visible evolution of the culture from random use of shallow caves to the construction of pithouses in the valley and atop the nearby mesas. About 900 A.D., the people began to utilize the "southern" architecture of multi-storied structures. From that point on, the Hovenweep people advanced to domesticated crops and fauna, such as the wild turkey, and extended their lifestyle to include arts and crafts—jewelry, costuming, pottery, ceremonial items, practical utensils, and items of dress.

The traveler to this remote spot in Utah will discover how an Anasazi "outpost" thrived through time. But one can also learn how they protected themselves against those who might threaten their wealth and sustenance, ranging from water resources to terraced farming areas.

Near Blanding, the traveler will find the Mule Canyon ruins, which were discovered as a construction crew was excavating ground for UT 95. This is a Bureau of Land Management site, relatively small by Four Corners standards, but the BLM has built trails and restrooms, and has covered part of the site with a roof. Nearby, on the rim of the canyon, there are ruins of several towers thought to be connected to the small settlement below. The BLM has not, as yet, made access to the upper site easy or possible, so the towers are largely off-limits.

One most impressive series of ruins—more than 200 have been located —is found at Natural Bridges National Monument, about 40 miles west of Blandings on UT 95. The monument is open year-round with some restrictions—it's closed during rainy times or winter snows—and there is a fee for admission charged during summer months. This a park for hiking, learning, and viewing, but visitors are not allowed to enter the variety of ruins. The monument enforces the strict, protective laws regarding such sites.

The Westwater Ruin is also located near Blanding, off of UT 163. Here, on Navajo land, the traveler will find a dwelling with five kivas. The Anasazi ruin reveals that the site was occupied perhaps five different times, the latest occurring at about 1300 A.D. Evidence indicates that the people who lived here were primarily farmers.

Visiting the site may involve some negotiation, since the access road crosses privately owned land. It is suggested that, when in Blanding, a stop at the local BLM office is helpful. Near Monticello, south on U.S. 163 to Montezuma Road, there is four-wheel-drive access to another small village regulated and preserved by the BLM. This one was apparently occupied at three different times between 900 A.D and 1300 A.D., and it contains three kivas.

Blanding is very much at the center of many Anasazi locations of the

Colorado Plateau, and from here the traveler can visit many parks, monuments, and sites open to public view. As well as a BLM office, there is a museum in the town. Edge of the Cedars Museum (660 West 400 North) is an educational experience as well as a source of information regarding the location of many of these sites. In fact, the nearby Edge of the Cedars Historical Monument houses an Anasazi ruin.

Other sites include the Grand Gulch Archaeological Primitive Area, Alkali Ridge, the Anasazi State Historical Monument, the Arch Canyon ruin, Big Westwater ruin, Canyonlands National Park, and Zion National Park.

ROCK ART

"Rock art" or petroglyphs can be viewed at a number of locations in Utah. These sites offer fascinating, artistic links to the past and, as such, deserve our utmost respect. Defacing the art or adding graffiti is never acceptable behavior. In most places to do so is in fact regarded as criminal behavior—and rightly so.

An Anasazi ruin, part of the Edge of the Cedars National Monument.

Although science is closing in on technology that can date some drawings—and can even identify motifs belonging to particular tribal traditions—many petroglyphs cannot yet be accurately ascribed to a time or an era. Many are thought to date from a period long before the Anasazi people entered the area.

Among the Great Basin peoples were those who were hunters and fishermen, but they were also quite resourceful when it came to finding natural foods in the dry, sparsely vegetated region that is now Utah. As surface water-levels rose and fell, the "written" accounts on the shoreside cliffs or rock faces were washed and rewashed with calcium and a saline solution that can be dated. As a result, we believe that some of the drawings may be as old as 10,000 years.

Fremont Indian State Park, near Richmond on U.S. 70, was created to preserve an Indian culture that we have not discussed—in part because of our relative ignorance when it comes to those people called "Fremont and Sevier Fremont" Indians. They were Great Basin people who adopted many of the Anasazi cultural aspects, including pithouses, adobe

Utah is home to numerous rock art sites, such as these Sand Island petroglyphs.

dwellings, and painted pottery, but they were not of the same linguistic family. They also had their own artistic and sculptural styles. The state park provides the visitor with three interpretive trails, a museum, and a visitor center. All seek to educate the traveler about this relatively small enclave of a millennium ago—including visits to archaeological and rock art sites.

Arches National Park, south of Moab on U.S. 163, includes a number of impressive petroglyphs (designs engraved on rock surfaces) and pictographs (pictures painted on the rock). One pictograph entitled "Courthouse Wash Panel" contains very large drawings—some over five feet high. There is an admission charge to the park, but there is also a visitor center where documentation is available. Unfortunately, this is one of the many sites that has been partially destroyed over the years by malicious visitors.

At Dinosaur National Monument, one finds art that falls into the 10,000-year-old bracket as well as art produced by more recent inhabitants. There are many petroglyphs within the monument's boundaries, as well as the famous "dinosaur quarry." Travelers interested in prehistoric art

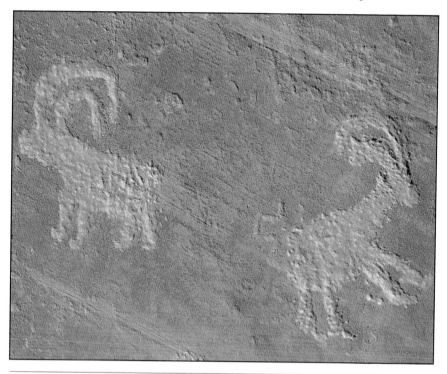

Bighorn sheep and a famous mastodon are among the many petroglyphs found near Moab.

can obtain maps from the quarry's visitor center.

Canyonlands National Park provides the traveler access to a variety of petroglyphs and pictographs. One of the most fascinating elements here is a wall devoted almost entirely to an array of hand-prints, pictographic recordings of both outlined hand prints and those traced and then painted. It's intriguing to compare the number of lefthand prints with the number of righthand prints and pairs.

Capitol Reef National Park, located on UT 24 between Hanksville and Torry, also includes the Fishlake National Forest and Dixie National Forest. It's a long way off the beaten track, but the petroglyphs are memorable and the visitor center does a fine job of recounting their history.

Other petroglyphic or pictographic sites include Newspaper Rock at Indian Creek State Park (near Monticello); Thompson Wash (near Thompson); Parowari Gap (near Cedar City); Ninemile Canyon (near Price); and Sand Island (near Bluff)

The vast majority of the dwellings and artwork are found in the area that the Utah Department of Tourism calls "Canyonland." For additional information about the area, which also includes the Glen Canyon

Although Capitol Reef National Park is far off the beaten track, it is well worth a visit.

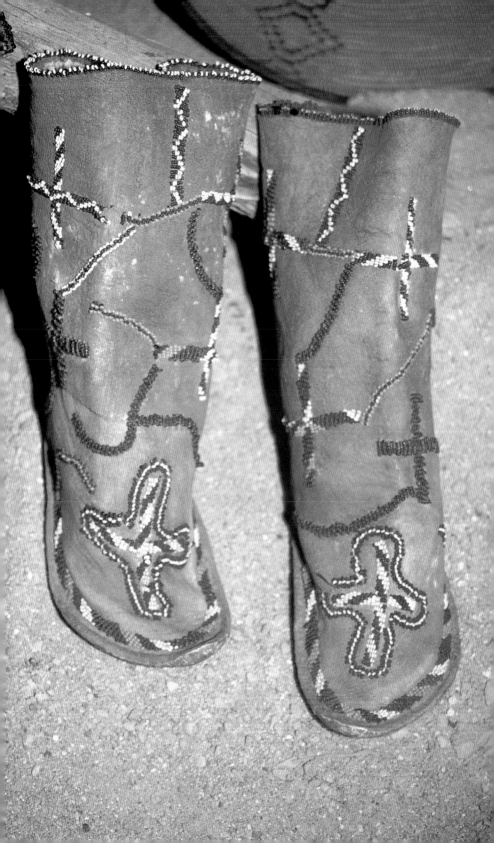

National Recreation Area, write the northern office in Moab (805 N. Main, Moab 84532) or call 801-259-8825 or 800-635-6622). You can also write the southern office in Monticello (117 S. Main, P.O. Box 490, Monticello 84535) or call 801-587-2425.

NAVAJO CULTURE

The Dineh people have considered part of Utah their homeland for centuries, and the Navajo Nation's northwestern border is the San Juan River where it meets the Colorado River. The Utah connection ends just a few miles above the Glen Canyon Dam in Page, AZ. For many non-Indians, that small slice of Utah includes what is possibly the most recognizable part of the Navajo Nation's three-state reservation: Monument Valley.

Hollywood's great director John Ford and Western actor John Wayne made this area part of the traveler's vision of the Southwest, but the region has been part of Native American culture since the waters receded from the land aeons ago. The Monument Valley Navajo Tribal Park is centered within this historic and glorious landscape near the park's

LEFT: Apache moccasins crafted in Utah.

entrance (just off U.S. 163), and this spot basically marks the state lines of Utah and Arizona. The traveler should not be confused by this, for Monument Valley, like the Painted Desert, is a region that defines its own boundaries fundamentally from Arizona's Black Mesa and Kaventa (junction of U.S. 160 and 163) to the San Juan River in Utah.

Travelers can access the area through the Navajo Tribal Park, or by taking a straight drive on 163 through the valley. There are also accesses at Oljeto and Goulding's Trading Post, both of which are western extensions of the tribal park's entrance road. For more extensive exploratory trips into the countryside, it is suggested that the traveler make arrangements for a tour given by an experienced guide in a four-wheel-drive vehicle. Even if you consider yourself a veteran off-road driver, remember that this is reservation land, and permits are generally required of all explorers who are not citizens of the Navajo Nation.

Although we have spent considerable time discussing the Dineh people in the Arizona and New Mexico chapters, it's worthwhile to recall key elements of Dineh history. One significant fact to remember is that the geographical core of the people's spiritual homeland lies between the San Juan River in the north—located in present-day Utah—and the Little Colorado in Arizona. Anyone who has traveled through this area understands that it is not a gentle environment, nor a promise for an easy life.

The Dineh were actually immigrants in an area already populated by a range of established nationalities. There were what we call the Anasazi, the Mogollon, the Hohokam, and their descendants, including the Pai people as well as visitors from the Pacific Coast and Mezo-America.

Grasping for historical straws can be both entertaining and risky, but let us venture into that territory for a moment. If it's accurate to say that the Dineh came to the Colorado Plateau about 1,000 years ago, they may have been hard-pressed to find land than no one else was willing to fight and die for. The Hopi had staked out their claim, as well as the Zuni and other Pueblo peoples, as had the Pai people and the Uto-Aztecan groups who inhabited the Great Basin and the western slopes of the Rockies.

It doesn't take a great sociological leap to understand that the "newcomer on the block" is generally assigned property that nobody else wants or that has no special value. Here is where Monument Valley takes on special significance, for it may well have represented a foot in the door for the Navajos, who would later dominate the entire Four Corners region. Monument Valley is a lovely place, but so is the Antarctic when seen via

Navajo Twins Bluff, Utah.

photographs. One need only travel to the Navajo National Monument in Arizona, just south of Kayenta, to see how quickly and how well these Indians from the Pacific Northwest adapted to their new environment.

Just as the European settlers lived different lives once they had landed on this continent, the Navajo people changed in their new homeland. "Navajo" is a Pueblo term that simply refers to the area of land in which the people lived, translating roughly as "over there, where the sun sets and nobody else lives." The Dineh, or "Earth People," tolerate the definition in much the same way that the Sioux accept the generic term that neighbors assigned to the Lakota, Nakota, and Dakota peoples, as well as many other tribal groups.

The Hopi had a more graphic description of the folks (both Spanish

A Navajo loom, displayed at Edge of the Cedars.

and native) that moved into their neighborhood, calling linguistically different, aggressive, and anti-social invaders "Tasavuh"—basically the Hopi word for "people who bash in enemies' skulls with rocks." Needless to say, neither the Dineh nor the Spanish chose to describe themselves in this manner to the outside world.

It is safe to say that the Dineh established themselves within just a couple of centuries as the dominant power on the Colorado Plateau. While there is no need to repeat their history in detail, it is interesting to note that the area we now call Monument Valley served as the foundation for what would become a very powerful structure. Thus, there is an important chapter of Navajo history that has to do with Utah, but there are several other significant groups who still maintain their homes in that state.

UTE CULTURE

As mentioned in the opening paragraphs of this section, the state's name is derived from the wide-ranging presence of the Ute people. Even though the name actually refers more to the group's historic high-altitude life, the Ute are also most closely associated with the culture of the Great Basin peoples, such as the Paiute and the Shoshone. All spoke dialects originating from the Uto-Aztecan family of languages.

The Ute people found ample cover in mountain ranges, and their territory extended from what is now called the Continental Divide east to the northern banks of the San Juan River in New Mexico and north to the Sevier River in west-central Utah—and even into southern Wyoming. For the most part, the Ute lived in small bands, groups that might gather together for a winter or join in a traditional "rabbit drive." Because they were hunters, among the most respected members of the tribe were those who fashioned spear and arrow points. Some creations were tiny, amazingly perfect arrowheads, smaller than a child's fingernail and used to hunt birds, small mammals, and fish. The small bands also designated their own leaders and shamans.

It is generally thought that the ferocity of the Ute, Apache, and Navajo peoples played a significant role in the disappearance of the Anasazi. However, one must not neglect the powerful effect of the 25-year drought that ended in 1300—the year that most experts estimate was the time when the Anasazi villages and outposts were finally deserted. Nonetheless, it is conceivable that the people with whom the Ute and other relatively nomadic tribes traded furs, hides, bone, and minerals were especially vulnerable to hostility during the drought years.

Three centuries later, there would be no question as to why the peaceful Pueblo people and other tribes were attacked: horses had been introduced by the Spanish into the southern, accessible regions. Given the horse, the Ute—like the Apache and, to a lesser degree, the Navajo—found their lifestyle greatly enhanced. They now had a means of crossing the Great Divide to do battle with the Arapaho.

For the most part, though, the Ute remained isolated in their vast territory of ranges, rivers, peaks, and valleys. The Ute did not have to deal with the reality of encroachment until the mid-19th century. First they dealt with the miners in Colorado and the troops and traders that followed; then they were faced with the Mormons in Utah, as well as wagon trains heading for California.

The key Ute leader at the time was a chief named Ouray, who rivals other great chiefs such as Tecumseh and Pontiac. Chief Ouray spoke English, Spanish, and several non-Uto-Aztecan languages, and he had learned the ways of the U.S. legal system. He gained respect through the years because of his ability to negotiate with non-Indian powers. Like Tecumseh, however, all of his intelligence and capabilities were done in by military actions.

Negotiations between U.S. Secretary of the Interior Carl Schurz and Chief Ouray took place while militant Generals Sheridan and Sherman waited in the wings, eager to attack. A truce and treaty were effected, but Ouray died one year later. He was 46 years old. After his death, the band was moved from its homeland to what is now the Uintah and Ouray Reservation near Vernal, Utah. It is undoubtedly the nation's most strangely-configured reservation.

The reservation is bordered on its east by Sweetwater Canyon, and on the west by Desolation Canyon. The northern border butts against the High Uintas Wilderness Area of the Uintah Mountains. The northern sector looks like the outline of Lake Superior. U.S. 40 runs through it, and there are numerous towns along the way to U.S. 19 at Heber City. The Wasatch National Forest forms the northwestern border of the reservation.

The 2500 square-mile reservation is found in what the Utah Department of Tourism calls "dinosaur land" and is headquartered in Fort Duchesne (P.O. Box 190, Ft. Duchesne 84026; 801-722-5141). The reservation sponsors an annual Bear Dance in April, and a Northern Ute Powwow and Rodeo in July.

Only a very small section of the Ute Mountain Indian Reservation crosses into Utah at the Four Corners intersection. However, the traveler can establish a Ute connection in southern Utah at Blanding, by contacting the Allen Canyon Ute Council (P.O. Box 916, Blanding 84511). There are also two other groups in the state that are associated with the Ute peoples. The traveler can locate the Goshute, south of Salt Lake City on UT 199, on the Skull Valley Indian Reservation, by contacting the group in Grantsville (P.O. Box 485, Grantsville 84029; 801-250-5911) or by contacting the central office of the Uintah and Ouray Reservation. Another Goshute tribal office is located In Ibapah (801-578-3419).

PAIUTE CULTURE

Like their Uto-Aztecan "cousins," the Paiute were historically a far-ranging tribe whose territory included parts of what is now Oregon, Idaho, California, Nevada, Utah, and Arizona. In their language, "Paiute" can mean either "true Ute" or "Ute of the water."

The Paiute were foragers, hunters, and fisherfolk, and were quite nomadic in their search for sustenance. They called their easily-assembled dwellings "wickiups," building them of a few rough branches covered with brush and weeds.

The Paiute of the Great Basin were highly resourceful. In the spring they harvested the tender shoots of the cattail and other roots and greens. Where these vegetables existed there were also migrations of ducks, and these waterfowl became part of the menu. In many places, spawning fish were fundamental to the Paiute diet. By summer, there were deer and smaller mammals as well as berries and rice grass, the latter providing seeds that were ground into meal powder. Pinon nuts were harvested in the autumn, and migrating creatures sometimes became part of Paiute larders for the approaching winters. Snakes, lizards, grubs, and certain other insects were not staples, but were not wasted or ignored. Non-Indians called the Paiute, the Ute, and other resourceful people "Digger Indians" because they seemed to be extracting food from the earth that would keep the people alive.

The northern Paiute people tended to react to intrusion and incursion more actively than their southern counterparts, perhaps because the vast resources of the northern region merited a more vigorous defense than the desert "wasteland" found in the southern part of the Great Basin. Also, after explorers, travelers, wagon trains, and troops encountered the Grand

Canyon, they faced dry mountains and expansive valleys like Death Valley, so the southern route was not the favored one.

However, the southern branch of the tribe played a special role in what might be called "the last significant violence" between Indians and non-Indians in the West, in 1888. A Nevada Paiute named Wovoka founded a religion called the "Ghost Dance." Son of a shaman, Wovoka had a vision during a solar eclipse. He proclaimed that the earth would soon be destroyed, and that it would then be reborn. A great prairie would evolve, and to this sea of grass the buffalo would return. The non-Indian would no longer exist, and all Indians—dead and alive—would become caretakers of the New World.

Wovoka advocated abandonment of all non-Indian ways, especially alcohol, and sought universal peace between all Indian peoples. He was not the first to preach this message. Tecumseh delivered the same plea, while his brother, Tenskwatawa, provided the spiritual impetus for the unification of Native Americans and the renunciation of European influences. And in 1680, a Pueblo spiritual and war leader had successfully planned a revolution that pushed the Spanish to El Paso and sought to

The butterfly basket, an example of Paiute artistry.

ban all European technology and thinking from the Southwest.

In each case, the non-Indians objected violently. The reaction to Wovoka's message was no different. The Indian visionary led others in special meditation, a host of prayers, and incessant chanting. The key element was the dancing of the "Ghost Dance." The dance became a rallying point among many tribes, for it promised a new and perfect existence. Its influence extended into the Dakotas, where the Sioux eventually donned Ghost Dance shirts, thought to protect them against bullets, and its practice there resulted in the tragic Wounded Knee massacre in 1890.

The Ghost Dance, like the forthcoming American Indian Church, would come to represent opposition or "return to the past" movements that non-Indians feared might trigger a massive Indian war. Since the army could not control the people in this respect, non-Indians charged missionaries, trading posts, reservation school systems, and federal bureaucrats with quashing all such activities.

While the Kaibab-Paiute Reservation is located on the Arizona-Utah border and has a tribal office in Fredonia, AZ, a Paiute Tribe of Utah center is located in Cedar City, Utah (512 S. Main St., 84720; 801-586-1111).

SHOSHONE CULTURE

Utah can lay claim to a small but significant portion of Shoshone history.

Although numerous heroic and significant contributions to native history were made by women, the average non-Indian asked for names of these women will be hard-pressed. In all likelihood, Pocahontas will be recalled first; after some thought or prodding, perhaps Sacajawea will also be mentioned. A Shoshone woman who served as guide, interpreter, and diplomat for the Lewis and Clark Expedition, Sacajawea could from one perspective be blamed for opening Western native territories to exploitation. It is, however, unfair to judge her in that harsh light.

Consider instead the strength, integrity, and intelligence Sacajawea demonstrated when asked to complete an unexpected and dangerous task. U.S. President Thomas Jefferson had purchased land from France, which had previously purchased the area from Spain and had no idea what to do with it. The history books call Jefferson's transaction the "Louisiana Purchase," and it was a remarkable bargain—nearly one million square miles were acquired for about $15 million.

Jefferson asked his personal secretary, Meriwether Lewis, to "audit" the newest addition to the country. Lewis, in turn, asked his best friend

William Clark to help him chart the way West. In 1804, the Lewis and Clark Expedition left St. Louis with 29 men who began moving up the Missouri River in the spring. The passage was so time-consuming that the group ended up spending the winter among the Mandan. Here they met a French-Canadian trader, Toussaint Charbonneau, who had just purchased a Shoshone woman from the nearby Hidatsa tribe. She had arrived as a slave of the Gros Ventre, who had held her captive for four years before exchanging her for goods with the Hidatsa.

There is no question that the expedition would have failed without Sacajawea. Over the next two years, she led the party to the Pacific Ocean and back to St. Louis. The fact that only one man was lost during this dangerous mission is a tribute to Sacajawea's ability to negotiate passage with more than 50 tribal groups encountered by the expedition. She also persuaded her own people to provide horses so the explorers could cross the Great Divide.

There is historical controversy regarding the last years of this exceptional woman's life. Some say she died in 1812, while other sources believe she lived until 1855. In any case, the journals of Lewis and Clark indicate that Sacajawea was among the most significant forces in non-Indian exploration of the continent, and in the shaping of a nation.

The Shoshone were not so hospitable half a century later, when the Bear River Shoshone, led by Chief Bear Hunter, fought the railroads, the telecommunications companies, the Mormon settlers, and the U.S. Army. In 1863, a military campaign was launched against the Shoshone, and the group was overwhelmingly defeated. When the resultant treaty was signed, the fight for the Great Basin had essentially ended. By 1869, the "golden spike' was driven at Promontory Point, Utah, thus marrying the east and west coasts by rail. The spike was hammered into a spot within former Shoshone territory.

Today, the Shoshone share one Utah reservation with Arapaho people and live in two others called "Goshute." There are also Shoshone reservations in Idaho, Nevada, and California, but the Shoshone are nevertheless regarded as one of the most economically deprived groups in the nation.

Utah's primary reservations are governed by the Goshute Business Council (P.O. Box 6104, Ibapah, 84034; 801-234-1138). There is also a tribal office in Brigham City, representing the Northwest Band of the Shoshone (660 South Second St. West, Brigham City, 84302; telephone, 801-723-7156).

CONCLUSION

There are many parallels to be drawn between the native history of Utah and that of Colorado. Both evidence a rich heritage of ancient and early post-European native culture. Both offer a number of sites accessible to the contemporary traveler. However, the ancient cultures of the Great Basin were quite different from those of the Anasazi and their ancestors on the Colorado Plateau.

Today, the traveler seeking Native America in Utah will discover more of the past than either the present or the future; yet the cultures of the Ute and the Navajo are very much alive.

MUSEUMS, ARCHIVES, AND CULTURAL CENTERS

Edge of the Cedars State Park (660 W. 400, North Blanding) offers an Anasazi Indian museum and ruin, and has one of the largest Anasazi pottery collections in the Southwest.

College of Eastern Utah Prehistoric Museum (155 E. Main, Price) has one of the world's best collections of dinosaur tracks, a rare dinosaur egg, skeletons, and a prehistoric Indian exhibit.

Dan O'Laurie Museum (118 E. Center, Moab) has prehistoric Indian artifacts on exhibit, a rock and mineral collection, and a mining display.

Monticello Museum (80 N. Main, Monticello) has Anasazi and pioneer collections.

Old Courthouse Museum (90 E. Center, Beaver) offers displays of pioneer and Indian artifacts.

MONUMENTS, HISTORIC SITES, AND PARKS

Anasazi State Park (Highway 12, Boulder) features a museum and Anasazi Indian village.

Arches National Park (25 miles south of I-70, just off U.S. 191 and 5 miles north of Moab) features one of the greatest concentrations of natural stone arches in the world.

Blanding, a community that is the gateway to the "Trail of the Ancients," offers road tours of ancient Indian sites.

Bluff, southeastern Utah's oldest community, features sandstone homes, St. Christopher's Mission, the swinging bridge across the San Juan River, a boat launch, and panels of Anasazi Indian petroglyphs.

Canyonlands National Park, Island in the Sky District (36 miles northwest of Moab via Highway 133) offers natural attractions including a high, broad mesa, elevation 6,000 to 6,500 feet; and the White Rim trail, a 100-mile, 4-wheel-drive route.

Canyonlands National Park, Maze District (46 miles off U-24, south of the Green River) features "The Great Gallery," a fine panel of Indian pictographs. Hiking trails and campsites are available.

Canyonlands National Park, Needles District (49 miles northwest of Monticello on Highway 211) passes through Newspaper Rock State Park and Indian Creek Canyon.

Capitol Reef National Park (on U-24, two hours southwest of the Green River) displays colorful cliffs and hiking trails that lead to natural bridges, hidden canyons, and ancient Indian petroglyphs.

Dry Fork Canyon (on the lower west portion of the Red Cloud Loop north of Vernal) is home to impressive Indian petroglyph panels.

Fremont Indian State Park (junction of Highway 89 and Interstate 70, 24 miles southwest of Richfield and 15 miles east of I-15) features a large collection of Fremont Indian artifacts from nearby Five Fingers Hill.

Grand Gulch Primitive Area (45 miles southwest of Blanding on Hwy 261) is a wilderness canyon featuring Indian ruins and rock art panels.

Home of Jacob Hamblin (Santa Clara) pays tribute to a man who befriended Indians and helped settle the area in the 1850s.

Hovenweep National Monument (six miles off state road 262, near Mexican Hat) features six clusters of ancient Pueblo ruins that include multi-storied towers and houses, kivas, storage shelters, and check dams.

Iron Mission State Park (585 N. Main, Cedar City) has a collection of horse-drawn vehicles and other pioneer items.

McConkie Ranch (ten miles from Vernal in Dry Fork Canyon) is a private ranch featuring two miles of extended petroglyphs on the canyon walls. Admission is charged.

Mexican Hat (U.S. 163) is named for the inverted stone sombrero visible on the east side of the highway. The formation is the entrance to the Navajo Indian Reservation and Monument Valley.

Montezuma Creek/Aneth Area (U-262) offers a panorama of ancient Anasazi culture and contemporary Navajo life.

Monument Valley Tribal Park (U.S. 163 at the Utah-Arizona line) is a mile-high monument on the Navajo Reservation.

Newspaper Rock State Historical Monument (13 miles off U-211) displays petroglyphs spanning 1,000 years and covering three distinct periods: prehistoric Indians, early Utes, and white settlers.

Nine Mile Canyon (35 miles northwest of Wellington) features canyon walls covered with petroglyphs and pictographs.

Rainbow Bridge National Monument is one of the seven natural wonders of the world, rising 309 feet above the stream below. It is large enough to span the Statue of Liberty. The monument can only be reached by boat tours from Lake Powell or by trail from the Navajo Trading Post.

CALENDAR OF EVENTS

APRIL
- Early in the month, the **Bear Dance** is performed at Fort Duchesne.

JULY
- An **Indian Rodeo** takes place at Fort Duchesne on the first weekend of the month.
- Late in the month the **Sun Dance** is performed at the Uintah and Ouray Reservation, Duchesne.
- The **Ute Stampede**, one of the state's best-known and longest-running rodeos, is also held in July, in Nephi.

SEPTEMBER
- On the second weekend, an **Indian Rodeo** is held at Fort Duchesne.

LIBRARIES
Southern Utah University Library (351 W. Center, Cedar City) features Paiute Indian artifacts in its special collections division.

Utah State Historical Society Library in Salt Lake City offers resource materials that cover the history of Utah, Mormons, Indians, and the West.

Ute Tribal Museum Library in Fort Duchesne houses a collection of books on Ute Indians.

CAMPGROUNDS
Campsites are available on the **Uintah and Ouray Reservation**, located in northeast Utah.

NATIVE AMERICAN CENTERS

Centers providing services to Native Americans in Utah include:
Salt Lake City Indian Health Center
Utah Native American Consortium, Inc. in Salt Lake City

NEWSPAPERS AND NEWSLETTERS

Native American newspapers and newsletters in Utah include: *Eagle's Eye*, BYU, Provo; *Indian Affairs News*, BYU, Provo; *Indian Liahona*, Salt Lake City; the newsletter of **POYE-DA AICADA**, Salt Lake City; the newsletter of **St. Christopher's Mission**, Bluff; and the *Ute Bulletin*, Fort Duchesne.

STATE AND REGIONAL ASSOCIATIONS

Utah Division of Indian Affairs in Salt Lake City acts as a liaison between tribes and the state.

Utah Navajo Development Council in Blanding works with the Navajo Reservation to provide health, education, natural resource, and housing services.

TOURISM OFFICES

For tourism information in Utah, contact the **Moab Visitor's Center** (805. N. Main, Moab); the **San Juan County Visitor's Center** (117 S. Main St., Monticello; 801-587-3235 or 800-574-4FUN); or the **Thompson Information Center**, (45 miles west of the Colorado state line, on I-70; 801-285-2234).

NATIVE UTAH

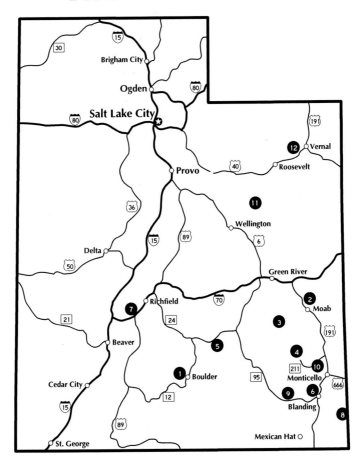

Selected Attractions:

SOURCES AND SELECTED RESOURCES

In the process of visiting many of the sites and locations for ORIGINS:THE SOUTH-WEST, there were numerous literary and historical works consulted, confronted, engaged, and utilized. Similarly, there were many publications that fall within the accessible public domain of libraries and, for example, the national park system. Wherever it seemed appropriate, notations were made along the narrative way. However, there is no doubt that the depth of research and education was aided by many of the following texts, either directly or indirectly. While it is not the author's role to evaluate the value or the validity of sources, it is certainly the traveler's prerogative to explore and examine the many different resources available—you are the final judge as to what is useful, what is mundane, and what is either outdated or inapplicable.

Ancient Cities of the Southwest: A Practical Guide to the Major Prehistoric Ruins of Arizona, New Mexico, Utah, and Colorado, by Buddy Mays, Chronicle Books, 1982.

Masked Gods: Navajo and Pueblo Ceremonialism, by Frank Waters, Sage/Swallow - Chicago, 1950.

Native Peoples of the Colorado Plateau, Museum of Northern Arizona, 1992.

A Visitor's Guide to Arizona's Indian Reservations, by Boye De Mente, Phoenix Books, 1988.

Hidden Southwest: Arizona, New Mexico, Southern Utah, Southern Colorado, Ulysses Press, 1992.

The Colorado, by Frank Waters, Swallow Press, 1946.

Book of the Hopi, by Frank Waters, Viking, 1963.

The Navajo, by Clyde Kluckhorn and Dorothea Leighton, Doubleday-Anchor, 1962.

The Book of the Navajo, by Raymond Locke, Mankind Publishing, 1992.

The American Heritage Book of Indians, by William Brandon with an introduction by John F. Kennedy, Dell, 1973.

Insights Guides: Native America, ed. by John Gattuso, APA Publications, 1992.

Anasazi: Ancient People of the Rock, by Donald Pike, Harmony Books, 1974.

Reference Encyclopedia of the American Indian, ed. by Barry Klein, Todd Publications, 1990.

The World of the American Indian, ed. by Jules Billard, National Geographic Society, 1974

Colorado: Big Mountain Country, by Nancy Wood, Doubleday, 1969.

Beneath These Red Cliffs: An Ethnohistory of the Utah Paiutes, by Ronald Holt, University of New Mexico Press, 1992.

The Spell of New Mexico, ed. by Tony Hillerman, University of New Mexico Press, 1976.

America's Ancient Treasures, by Franklin Folsom and Mary Folsom, University of New Mexico Press, 1983.

Atlas of the North American Indian, by Carl Waldman, Facts on File Publications, 1985.

Encyclopedia of Native American Tribes, by Carl Waldman, Facts on File Publications, 1988.

Native American Directory, Native American Cooperative, 1982.

Indian America: A Traveler's Companion, by Eagle/Walking Turtle, John Muir Publications, 1989.

A Guide to America's Indians, by Arnold Marquis, University of Oklahoma Press, 1974.

Only in Santa Fe, by Susan Haza-Hammond, Voyageur Press, 1992.

Acoma: Pueblo in the Sky, by Ward Alan Migre, University of New Mexico Press, 1991.

Collecting the West, by Ketchum William, Crown Publishing, 1993.

MAGAZINES AND OTHER PUBLICATIONS

Navajo Times
Arizona's Indian Country
Indian Trader's Western and Indian Arts and Crafts
Dine 'Bi ' Keyah: Exploring the Navajo Spirit
Pinal Ways: Past and Present at Gila River Indian Cultural Center
SouthWest People
SouthWest Sampler
Eight Northern Pueblos
Indian Doings
Smithsonian
Native Peoples
National Geographic
New Mexico
Arizona Highways
National Parks

One will discover at almost every stop on the road—national park or monument, local information center, motels and shopping malls—many, many publications published by the myriad tourism attractions and traveler's destinations in the region. Many will have, at first glance, little to do with visiting Native American locales or sites. Most may have little connection, but is always rewarding to find some brochure, pamphlet, flyer or local newspaper that contains a nugget of information related to the Southwest's bountiful passports to Native America.

ABOUT THE AUTHOR

Hayward Allen's Western roots (by way of family) reach back to the 1880s. The author himself was born in Tennessee and raised in a variety of places—Virginia, Hawaii, California, Ohio. Allen also worked on ranches in Colorado and Wyoming as a youth. He graduated from the University of Colorado with his master's degree in 1962, then joined the Peace Corps and served in Harar, Ethiopia.

Allen has since been a teacher, editor, and arts critic; as the author of two volumes of the *Traveler's Guide to Native America*, he has demonstrated a remarkable empathy for America's first people and their cultures. He is also the author of a natural history book entitled *The Great Blue Heron*, and he now lives with one home in Arizona and the other in Wisconsin.